Navigating Cross-Cultural Missions

The Navigators
International Executive Team

Colorado Springs, Colorado

Navigating Cross-Cultural Missions

Contents

INTRODUCTION

Serving as a cross-cultural missionary, regardless of what position a person plays on the field, is a challenging and complex endeavor. To thrive and be fruitful, cross-cultural laborers need a deep understanding of what the Scriptures teach about this calling. As Navigators, we are passionate about the Scriptures. They provide us with God's living and timeless wisdom for every area of life, including missionary service.

Navigating Cross-Cultural Missions was developed by about thirty experienced Navigator leaders from around the globe. These international leaders have served as cross-cultural missionaries in rural villages, on secular campuses, in corporate offices, among the poor, and within every major religion. They know from experience what it takes to send and receive cross-cultural laborers. As a result, this study will expand your vision and understanding of the most critical issues facing Navigator missionaries today. In light of what's at stake, we believe the work you put into this study will be worthwhile.

PURPOSES OF THE STUDY

The Navigator Worldwide Partnership is advancing the Gospel in more than one hundred nations. Navigators around the world are preparing new missionaries in diverse ways. These include short-term missions opportunities, leadership development programs, fundraising training seminars, campus training, and other helpful efforts.

However, our international leaders have seen the need to help missionaries gain a deeper understanding of what the Scriptures reveal about cross-cultural service. This study is meant to fill that need, to be a vital resource that helps assure that our global missions efforts are founded on God's Word.

Although *Navigating Cross-Cultural Missions* addresses the most critical aspects of cross-cultural missions, this book is not meant to be an exhaustive course on missiology. We hope that it will inspire us into a life-long discovery of the Scriptures as they pertain to advancing the Gospel.

WHO SHOULD USE THE NCCM?

This book is designed for Navigators who are seriously considering or have already decided to pursue medium-term or long-term missions as a vocation. It is for people who have been or are in the process of being approved by regional or national leaders to work cross-culturally. In compiling the content, we assumed that participants would already have sufficient spiritual maturity and a demonstrated readiness for cross-cultural work.

The *primary* audience for the book is first-time cross-cultural laborers who are preparing to serve in new contexts. It's designed to be used before they are sent into service, to build a biblical framework for interpreting cross-cultural experiences before work on the field begins. The Holy Spirit and the Scriptures can bring clarity to strategic ministry questions as well as to the deep personal struggles that missionaries often face. It is better to raise and address these issues early in the sending process.

In addition, this study will benefit those who have been on the field for a few years. Once missionaries have had some first-hand experience and have a better knowledge of the cultural context, the study will help them evaluate and realign the ministry in light of what they are experiencing.

Finally, this study will serve veteran cross-cultural missionaries. As missionaries learn and grow from long-term experience on the field, God can use the Scriptures to speak in fresh and new ways.

Overview of the NCCM

There are three main sections in this book. The first section deals with our identity as Navigators—the unique characteristics of our Navigator Calling, Values, and Vision. This section also helps missionaries to consider, through the lens of the Scriptures, their God-designed identity and gifting, and to understand how that gifting fits in the new context where they will serve.

The second section deepens and enriches our understanding of the Gospel of the kingdom of Jesus—the message that we are called to speak and live. Section 2 also looks at the nature of Gospel movements; that is, how the Gospel penetrates a culture and produces spiritual generations.

The third section looks at what the Scriptures reveal about the essence of the church (*ekklesia*), the different cultural expressions of biblical church, and the relational nature of the church. This section also guides us into a deeper understanding of what it means to make disciples (Matthew 28:19-20) and the importance of helping people to grow in Christlikeness.

How to Use This Study

The book should be used in close collaboration between outgoing missionaries and their sending leaders or mentors; that is, interact regularly about this material with at least one mature believer who is part of the effort to prepare and send them. Experienced missionaries would also benefit by doing the study with a local leader or a ministry team. Ideally, a group of people would work on the study together. Learning and growth occur best in the context of close relationships.

Completing the study will take about forty hours. This includes time in personal study and time in discussion with the sending leader, mentor, or group. Here is a suggested step-by-step approach.

1. Hold an initial planning meeting: decide how often to meet, set the

proposed completion date, and determine how much material to cover before each meeting, etc.

2. Set aside sufficient time in your weekly schedule to prepare the assigned material. You can prepare individually or as a team.

3. Meet regularly with your leader/mentor to discuss your prepared study.

4. After the entire study has been completed, review and discuss its main points, and address unresolved questions.

ROLE OF THE LEADER/MENTOR

Sending missionaries is dependent on God's personal leading and the collaboration of the sending community and receiving team. It should be a highly relational process, as we see in the Scriptures. Leaders and mentors can play an important role in helping individuals, couples, and teams work through questions related to this major decision and calling. The leader's role in working with this study is to ask good questions, listen carefully, support and encourage, and identify practical needs during the sending process.

Ideally, *but not exclusively,* the leader or mentor for this study will be someone who A) has some cross-cultural experience and/or awareness of the strategic needs in the receiving region, and B) knows well the character, maturity, and gifting of the outgoing missionaries involved. Some basic skills in facilitating a study of the Scriptures is helpful, but no special training is required to lead people through this content.

Comments about and suggestions for improving future editions of this study can be sent to IETpublishing@navigators.org.

Serving with you,
Alan Ch'ng, Eddie Broussard, Neil Grindheim, and Glenn McMahan
Editorial Team

THE NAVIGATORS AND YOU

In this section, we will address two interconnected aspects of cross-cultural missions. First, it is important for our missionaries to understand the unique Calling, Values, and Vision that God has given to The Navigators. We are a diverse Worldwide Partnership working in more than one hundred countries. But we also share a common heritage and vision that unifies us as Navigators.

Second, this section is designed to help missionaries think carefully about personal gifting and calling. The goal here is to help you discern, with the Holy Spirit, how you can best serve in your cross-cultural ministry.

Let's first look more closely at our Navigator Calling, Values, and Vision—what we call "The Core." The Core expresses who we are as Navigators regardless of what part of the world we are from.

UNDERSTANDING THE NAVIGATOR CORE

Written by the Navigator International Leadership Community, The Core articulates the profound, God-given purposes of our Worldwide Partnership. It speaks to what we believe God has called us to do (our calling), what we hold dear to our hearts (our values), and what we envision for our future as God graciously blesses our efforts (our vision).

The Navigator movement, which today embraces many thousands of people, had small beginnings among youth and U.S. naval officers. In the 1950s, our founder, Dawson Trotman, used the term "reproducing reproducers" to describe our calling. He developed "The Wheel Illustration" to describe what we aspire to in our lives as followers of Jesus. In the 1970s, then President Lorne Sanny used the phrase, "To help fulfill Christ's Great Commission by multiplying laborers in every nation" to summarize the primary aim of The Navigators. Then we produced an important document titled "Fundamentals of Ministry" that described what we mean by "disciple" and "laborer" in ways that parallel our current values.

In the 1990s, we also produced the *Scriptural Roots of Our Ministry* (SRM). This helped us to think biblically about the kingdom of God as it pertains to our mission and calling in the world. The study sharpened our understanding of major biblical themes that included the purity and movement of the Gospel, the kingdom of God, and the people of God. It established the foundation for us to implement Gospel movements.

This emphasis on laying foundations for spiritual generations is a key aspect of our Navigator identity. As Navigators, we believe God will raise up foundational disciples who are committed to the Lord, to one another, and to the Navigator Core.

The outcome we all seek is to see successive generations of laborers that result in movements of the Gospel. We trust God together for this outcome. As Paul wrote in 1 Corinthians 3, we labor in God's field, each of us working to accomplish the tasks that the Lord has assigned us.

Discover More

We encourage you to read the Core at our public international website: www.navigatorsworldwide.org. We also recommend three short videos that portray the Navigator Calling, Values, and Vision. They are titled the "Drawing Out" series: https://vimeo.com/channels/navigatorsworldwide/videos.

GOD'S PROMISES AND THE NAVIGATORS

Who, really, would we be if we did not believe God's promises? His promises declare his grand and eternal purposes through history. They reveal what he is doing and what he will do in our world.

When we reflect and pray over the promises of God, it is not our faith that brings them to life. The fulfillment of his promises does not depend on our zeal to "claim the promises." Rather, the promises of God ignite our faith and shape our identity *as they claim us*. As that happens, we are caught up in the mighty river of God's purposes. The Navigator movement, from Dawson Trotman to this day, has been shaped by the promises of God—particularly the promises expressed through Isaiah.

Study 1: How God has Fulfilled and Will Fulfill His Promises

ISAIAH 49:1-6

Listen to me, you islands; hear this, you distant nations: Before I was born the Lord called me; from my mother's womb he has spoken my name. He made my mouth like a sharpened sword, in the shadow of his hand he hid me; he made me into a polished arrow and concealed me in his quiver. He said to me, "You are my servant, Israel, in whom I will display my splendor." But I said, "I have labored in vain; I have spent my strength for nothing at all. Yet what is due me is in the Lord's hand, and my reward is with my God." And now the Lord says—he who formed me in the womb to be his servant to bring Jacob back to him and gather Israel to himself, for I am honored in the eyes of the Lord and my God has been my strength—he says: "It is too small a thing for you to be my servant to restore the tribes of Jacob and bring back those of Israel I have kept. I will also make you a light for the Gentiles, that my salvation may reach to the ends of the earth."

ISAIAH 54:1-4

"Sing, barren woman, you who never bore a child; burst into song, shout for joy, you who were never in labor; because more are the children of the desolate woman than of her who has a husband," says the Lord. "Enlarge the place of your tent, stretch your tent curtains wide, do not hold back; lengthen your cords, strengthen your stakes. For you will spread out to the right and to the left; your descendants will dispossess nations and settle in their desolate cities.

Isaiah 60:21-61:11

"Then all your people will be righteous and they will possess the land forever. They are the shoot I have planted, the work of my hands, for the display of my splendor. The least of you will become a thousand, the smallest a mighty nation. I am the Lord; in its time I will do this swiftly."

The Spirit of the Sovereign Lord is on me, because the Lord has anointed me to proclaim good news to the poor. He has sent me to bind up the brokenhearted, to proclaim freedom for the captives and release from darkness for the prisoners to proclaim the year of the Lord's favor and the day of vengeance of our God, to comfort all who mourn, and provide for those who grieve in Zion—to bestow on them a crown of beauty instead of ashes, the oil of joy instead of mourning, and a garment of praise instead of a spirit of despair. They will be called oaks of righteousness, a planting of the Lord for the display of his splendor.

They will rebuild the ancient ruins and restore the places long devastated; they will renew the ruined cities that have been devastated for generations. Strangers will shepherd your flocks; foreigners will work your fields and vineyards. And you will be called priests of the Lord, you will be named ministers of our God. You will feed on the wealth of nations, and in their riches you will boast. Instead of your shame you will receive a double portion, and instead of disgrace you will rejoice in your inheritance. And so you will inherit a double portion in your land, and everlasting joy will be yours.

"For I, the Lord, love justice; I hate robbery and wrongdoing. In my faithfulness I will reward my people and make an everlasting covenant with them. Their descendants will be known among the nations and their offspring among the peoples. All who see them will acknowledge that they are a people the Lord has blessed." I delight greatly in the Lord; my soul rejoices in my God. For he has clothed me with garments of salvation and arrayed me in a robe of his righteousness, as a bridegroom adorns his head like a priest, and as a bride adorns herself with her jewels. For as the soil makes the sprout come up and a garden causes seeds to grow, so the Sovereign Lord will make righteousness and praise spring up before all nations.

Discover More

Other key Navigator promises include: Isaiah 42:1-8 and Isaiah 55:1-13. For further study on how God's promises function in the lives of God's people, read Galatians 3:6-29; Psalm 119:116, 123, 148; 2 Corinthians 1:18-20; 1 Peter 1:10-12; Genesis 12:1-3; Romans 4:16-21.

Think Deeper

1.1 How do these promises shape your understanding of what God is calling us to believe today? How do they help shape your thinking about what God wants to do through you?

1.2 List promises that God has impressed on you. Can you see the correlation between the promises you listed and the experiences God has used to shape your life so far?

BIBLICAL BASIS FOR THE NAVIGATOR CORE

"To advance the Gospel of Jesus and his kingdom into the nations through spiritual generations of laborers living and discipling among the lost."

Understanding our Calling requires us to know the scriptures from which it originates. Let's look at each element of the Navigator Calling more closely.

Study 2: The Gospel, Jesus, and His Kingdom

"To advance the Gospel of Jesus and his kingdom . . ."

MARK 1:1

The beginning of the gospel about Jesus Christ, the Son of God . . .

ACTS 8:12

But when they believed Philip as he preached the good news of the kingdom of God and the name of Jesus Christ, they were baptized, both men and women.

ACTS 28:30-31

For two whole years Paul stayed there in his own rented house and welcomed all who came to see him. He proclaimed the kingdom of God and taught about the Lord Jesus Christ—with all boldness and without hindrance!

Discover More

For more on the Navigator Calling see Matthew 24:14; Act 20:24; 2 Corinthians 2:12; Ephesians 1:13; Ephesians 6:15; 1 Thessalonians 2:8; Revelation 14:6; Mark 4:1-34.

Think Deeper

2.1 How might you communicate "the kingdom" in your cultural setting?

CR

Study 3: God's Plan for the Nations

The biblical term for "nations" does not mean countries; rather, it means ethnicities. There are often many enthnicities within one country.

". . . into the nations . . ."

Genesis 12:1-3

The Lord had said to Abram, "Go from your country, your people and your father's household to the land I will show you. "I will make you into a great nation, and I will bless you; I will make your name great, and you will be a blessing. I will bless those who bless you, and whoever curses you I will curse; and all peoples on earth will be blessed through you."

Matthew 24:14

And this gospel of the kingdom will be preached in the whole world as a testimony to all nations, and then the end will come.

Revelation 5:9-10

And they sang a new song, saying: "You are worthy to take the scroll and to open its seals, because you were slain, and with your blood you purchased for God persons from every tribe and language and people and nation. You have made them to be a kingdom and priests to serve our God, and they will reign on the earth."

Matthew 28:16-20

Then the eleven disciples went to Galilee, to the mountain where Jesus had told them to go. When they saw him, they worshiped him; but some doubted. Then Jesus came to them and said, "All authority in heaven and on earth has been given to me. Therefore, go and make disciples of all nations, baptizing them in the name of the Father and of the Son and of the Holy Spirit, and teaching them to obey everything I have commanded you. And surely I am with you always, to the very end of the age."

Discover More

See also: Genesis 10:1-12; Acts 17:22-31; Deuteronomy 26:5; Isaiah 51:1-2; Galatians 3:6-9; Isaiah 11:1-12; Mark 11:15-17 (compare Isaiah 56:1-8); Acts 21:27-29 & 22:21-22 (compare with 1 Kings 8:41-43); Romans 2:17-24 (compare Ezekiel 36:16-23); Psalm 2; Psalm 22:27-31; Psalm 67; Psalm 96.

Think Deeper

3.1 How is the Gospel universal to all nations?

෪

Study 4: Generations and Laborers

Navigators get the term "laborer" from Matthew 9:37-38. "Generations" is prominent in the Bible, and is even rooted in the way God made the world.

"...through spiritual generations of laborers..."

MATTHEW 9:37-38

Then he said to his disciples, "The harvest is plentiful but the workers are few. Ask the Lord of the harvest, therefore, to send out workers into his harvest field."

GENESIS 1:11-12 (GENERATIONS IN NATURE)

Then God said, "Let the land produce vegetation: seed-bearing plants and trees on the land that bear fruit with seed in it, according to their various kinds." . . . The land produced vegetation: plants bearing seed according to their kinds and trees bearing fruit with seed in it according to their kinds. And God saw that it was good.

PSALM 78:1-7

My people, hear my teaching; listen to the words of my mouth. I will open my mouth with a parable; I will utter hidden things, things from of old—things we have heard and known, things our ancestors have told us. We will not hide them from their descendants; we will tell the next generation the praiseworthy deeds of the Lord, his power, and the wonders he has done. He decreed statutes for Jacob and established the law in Israel, which he commanded our ancestors to teach their children, so the next generation would know them, even the children yet to be born, and they in turn would tell their children. Then they would put their trust in God and would not forget his deeds but would keep his commands.

2 TIMOTHY 2:1-2

You then, my son, be strong in the grace that is in Christ Jesus. And the things you have heard me say in the presence of many witnesses entrust to reliable people who will also be qualified to teach others.

Think Deeper

4.1 What prompted Jesus to point to the critical need for laborers? What does it take for a person to become a laborer for the kingdom?

4.2 Our Calling says "to advance the Gospel . . . through spiritual generations of laborers." How might this affect your approach to cross-cultural work?

CR

Study 5: Living and Discipling among the Lost

Jesus sought to relate with people who didn't yet know him. "The Son of Man came to seek and to save what was lost" (Luke 19:10).

". . . living and discipling among the lost . . ."

Matthew 11:19

The Son of Man came eating and drinking, and they say, 'Here is a glutton and a drunkard, a friend of tax collectors and sinners.'"

Matthew 9:12-13

Jesus said, "It is not the healthy who need a doctor, but the sick. But go and learn what this means: 'I desire mercy, not sacrifice.' For I have not come to call the righteous, but sinners."

John 17:13-18

I am coming to you now, but I say these things while I am still in the world, so that they may have the full measure of my joy within them. I have given them your word and the world has hated them, for they are not of the world any more than I am of the world. My prayer is not that you take them out of the world but that you protect them from the evil one. They are not of the world, even as I am not of it. Sanctify them by the truth; your word is truth. As you sent me into the world, I have sent them into the world.

Discover More

For more about Jesus's heart for the lost, see Matthew 10:11-42; Matthew 13:24-43; Luke 15:1-31; John 15:16-27. To learn more from the Epistles, read 1 Corinthians 9:19-11:1; 2 Corinthians 5:14-7:2; Ephesians 4:17-6:20; Philippians 1:27-2:16; 1 Peter 2:9-3:17.

Think Deeper

5.1 What happens if we neglect either "living" or "discipling" and focus on only on one or the other?

5.2 In John 17 (above), Jesus calls us to be in the world, living among the lost. Explain why the word "among" is so important to disicpling.

OUR GOAL: SPIRITUAL GENERATIONS

Taken as a whole, The Core is our expression of God's assignment for The Navigators. The overarching outcome we seek together, around the world, is *multiplying ministries that produce spiritual generations.*

But how do we build multiplying ministries? Over our history, Navigator leaders have studied the Scriptures extensively to identify the primary factors that are needed for developing multiplying ministries. They discovered six "critical factors," and have developed them into a useful set of studies for our international work.

Titled *The Six Critical Factors for a Multiplying Ministry,* the studies serve as a framework that can be used to implement The Core. All six studies can be downloaded from the ILC website's resource page (www.ilcworldwide.org), or by contacting the International Office staff. Below is a brief summary of the six critical factors:

1. Laying Foundations: Where and how we begin our cross-cultural work determines what it will look like years later. This is clear, for example, in 1 Corinthians 3:10-11.

2. Going to the Lost: We are in the world, in part, for the sake of the lost (see John 17:14-21). We won't make real progress in a ministry unless we, each according to his or her role, are working together to reach the lost (see also 2 Corinthians 5:18-20).

3. Discipling our Generation: Our challenge is to disciple broken people (Isaiah 61:1-4), to see spiritual transformation occuring through the Word, the

Holy Spirit, and a Christ-centered community.

4. Community: It's difficult for disciples to grow without vibrant communities of believers. Personal growth takes place in the context of relationships, and healthy relationships bring glory to God (Ephesians 4:15-16).

5. Laborers and Leaders: Multiplying ministries constantly develop and nurture new leaders and laborers. This includes leaders who are pioneers, mobile alongsiders, local servants, and others. As we see in 1 Timothy 2:2, developing new leaders and laborers is essential to spiritual generations.

6. Spiritual Generations: Generational thinking is rooted in the promises of God, in the fact that God will advance his Gospel through the generations. A multiplying work will focus on this outcome and work toward this end. There is a difference between a fruitful ministry and a generational ministry.

Each of these six critical factors are addressed in *Navigating Cross-Cultural Missions*. You will be able to identify them as you proceed through the study. But we encourage you to download the study for each of the six factors.

YOUR CONTRIBUTION

Each person has a unique identity created by God and shaped by family and culture. As we consider cross-cultural missions, we should recognize the importance of each person's personality, strengths, giftings, and weaknesses. Everyone hopes to find the best possible fit between the person and the mission—for the sake of the individual, the team, and the work.

Questions about your contribution are deeper and more profound than just missionary job functions. They are related to each person's calling from God. "At some point every one of us confronts the question: How do I find and fulfill the central purpose of my life?" writes Os Guinness. "We desire to make a difference. We long to leave a legacy. . . . Our passion is to know that we are fulfilling the purpose for which we are here on earth." We hope this section plays a small role toward that end as you seek God's leading and direction.

SPIRITUAL GIFTING AND CROSS-CULTURAL MINISTRY

There are four major passages about spiritual gifts in the New Testament. Please take some time to read Romans 12:3-8; 1 Corinthians 12:1-14; Ephesians 4:7-13; and 1 Peter 4:10-11. In them we see a picture of a body, the Body of Christ, with interdependent functions.

Typically, people study the spiritual gifts as isolated traits. But it is healthier to consider them in broader contexts. Scripture teaches that believers are God's workmanship created for his purposes in the context of the Body of Christ. The Spirit distributes gifts to believers so that we can serve God's purposes.

Study 6: Your God-Given Design and Gifting

EPHESIANS 2:10

For we are God's handiwork, created in Christ Jesus to do good works, which God prepared in advance for us to do.

EPHESIANS 4:11-16

It was he who gave some to be apostles, the prophets, the evangelists, the pastors and teachers, to equip his people for works of service, so that the body of Christ may be built up until we all reach unity in the faith and in the knowledge of the Son of God and become mature, attaining to the whole measure of the fullness of Christ. Then we will no longer be infants, tossed back and forth by the waves, and blown here and there by every wind of teaching and by the cunning and craftiness of people in their deceitful scheming. Instead, speaking the truth in love, we will grow to become in every respect the mature body of him who is the head, that is, Christ. From him the whole body, joined and held together by every supporting ligament, grows and builds itself up in love, as each part does its work.

Think Deeper

6.1 How does your gifting relate to God's purposes, as well as to the specific needs within your cross-cultural ministry? Do you feel like there is a good fit?

SPIRITUAL GIFTS AND THE MATURING OF A MINISTRY

In Ephesians 4, Paul notes the gifts of apostle, prophet, evangelist, pastor and teacher. These are not the greatest gifts; they are functions beneficial for laying foundations on which healthy spiritual bodies become mature.

Study 7: Diversity in the Body of Christ

1 PETER 4:8-11

Above all, love each other deeply, because love covers over a multitude of sins. Offer hospitality to one another without grumbling. Each of you should use whatever gift you have received to serve others, as faithful stewards of God's grace in its various forms. If anyone speaks, they should do so as one who speaks the very words of God. If anyone serves, they should do so with the strength God provides, so that in all things God may be praised through Jesus Christ. To him be the glory and the power for ever and ever. Amen.

1 CORINTHIANS 12:4-11

There are different kinds of gifts, but the same Spirit distributes them. There are different kinds of service, but the same Lord. There are different kinds of working, but in all of them and in everyone it is the same God at work. Now to each one the manifestation of the Spirit is given for the common good. To one there is given through the Spirit a message of wisdom, to another a message of knowledge by means of the same Spirit, to another faith by the same Spirit, to another gifts of healing by that one Spirit, to another miraculous powers, to another prophecy, to another distinguishing between spirits, to another speaking in different kinds of tongues, and to still another the interpretation of tongues. All these are the work of one and the same Spirit, and he distributes them to each one, just as he determines.

Think Deeper

7.1 What relational qualities do teams need to function in unity and diversity?

THE FOUR CONTRIBUTIONS

As you prepare to move into your new cultural context, there is an important question to answer: What will be your specific contributions to the advance of the Gospel?

Contributions are different than positions and titles. For example, Erastus was the treasurer of Corinth (his position and title). He earned his income by conventional means. But what was his contribution to the advance of the Gospel? Timothy, on the other hand, had left his home town to accompany Paul in his travels. He was primarily, but not exclusively, supported by gift income. But what contribution did he make to the advance of the Gospel? Did this contribution ever change? Did he make more than one contribution? Identifying and understanding each of the contributions we see in the Scriptures can help you determine your own role and contribution.

The spread of the Gospel, from its early beginnings in Jerusalem and then into the nations, reveals several important "contributions" that were vital to progress. The Navigator International Leadership Community has identified at least four contributions in the Scriptures. We believe each is vital to advancing the Gospel generationally into the nations. The Four Contributions are:

- *Pioneering teams:* laborers and leaders who move into new contexts to plant the Gospel and to lay the foundations of a generational ministry
- *Local laborers:* "insiders" who serve within local relational networks in ways that are integrated into normal work and family life
- *Local leaders:* people who care for, lead, and build community among laborers in a local context
- *Mobile alongsiders:* leaders who travel to support local laborers and leaders, and pioneering teams

❧

Study 8: The Four Contributions in Thessalonica

Please read Acts 17:1-9 and all of 1 Thessalonians. Paul, Silas, and Timothy came as *pioneers* to Thessalonica. They were committed to planting the Gospel among local people. Later, believers began to serve as *local laborers,* as insiders in their own context. When Paul's letter was written, there were already *local leaders* to whom Paul refers as "those who work hard among you and are over you in the Lord." Paul also refers to Timothy's work to "strengthen and encourage" them in the faith. Timothy's contribution was to provide leadership as a *mobile alongsider.* We know that Paul and Timothy (as well as others like Titus and Tychicus) exercised a mobile alongsider function to support the local ministries that had been planted.

Discover More

Read about how the Gospel advanced in Philippi (Acts 16:11-40 and Philippians), and in Ephesus (Acts 19; Acts 20:13-38; Ephesians; 1 and 2 Timothy). Watch a short film about The Four Contributions at vimeo.com/116715363.

Think Deeper

8.1 How did these contributions relate to and complement each other? How might these insights inform and clarify your role as a missionary?

A Case Study

It's been over ten years since Mary and Philip moved to Southland to pioneer a ministry among the indigenous people of that country. They have loved people, served them, and openly shared their faith in ways that the local people could understand. They have seen many young people come to faith.

However, as the young people have started to work, get married, and have children, they have met less frequently with Mary and Philip. People know Mary and Philip, but they don't know each other very well. Community is weak.

Mary and Philip have decided to return to their sending country so their children can begin college. In six months you will be arriving in Southland as a cross-cultural missionary to replace Mary and Philip. In light of The Four Contributions, what role (or roles) are needed in this ministry context? How would you go about helping these contributions develop?

ASSESSING GOD'S WORK IN A REGION

As cross-cultural missionaries consider their personal identities and gifting, everyone hopes to find a good "fit" between the missionary, the team, and the needs on the field. Therefore, it is important to understand how God has been working in the region.

The Worldwide Partnership of The Navigators comprises a diverse array of new, developing, and mature ministries. We use a framework called "The Four Stages of Ministry" for thinking about each country's growth. They are:

- *Initiating* countries have an intentional Navigator work that is just beginning under the leadership of a Navigator pioneer.
- *Developing* countries have a foundational group of believers who are showing commitment to the Lord, to one another, and to The Core.
- *Maturing* countries have works led primarily by national leaders who are

implementing the Navigator Core and expanding into new contexts.

- Finally, *partnering* countries have nationally led ministries that are influential contributors to the Worldwide Partnership, including by sending cross-cultural missionaries.

Throughout the Bible, people sought a clear notion of their role in the context of what God was doing at the time. Jesus clearly understood the parameters and the focus of his work, and he knew when his work on earth was completed. Paul and other laborers in the New Testament sought God's leading to discern when they were finished with each phase of work. Understanding what the Scriptures teach about this issue will provide us with guidance.

Study 9: The Mission Parameters of Jesus and Paul

JOHN 17:4

I have brought you glory on earth by completing the work you gave me to do.

ROMANS 15:17-24

Therefore, I glory in Christ Jesus in my service to God. I will not venture to speak of anything except what Christ has accomplished through me in leading the Gentiles to obey God by what I have said and done—by the power of signs and wonders, through the power of the Spirit of God. So from Jerusalem all the way around to Illyricum, I have fully proclaimed the gospel of Christ. It has always been my ambition to preach the gospel where Christ was not known, so that I would not be building on someone else's foundation. . . . But now that there is no more place for me to work in these regions, and since I have been longing for many years to visit you, I plan to do so when I go to Spain. I hope to see you while passing through and to have you assist me on my journey there, after I have enjoyed your company for a while.

1 CORINTHIANS 3:10

By the grace God has given me, I laid a foundation as a wise builder, and someone else is building on it. But each one should build with care.

Discover More

The New Testament account of Ephesus takes place over about thirty-five years from Paul's journey to Ephesus (53-57 AD) until Revelation (90 AD). You can read about this process in Acts 19:1-10 and Acts 20:17-38; all of 1 Timothy; and Revelation 2:1-7.

Think Deeper

9.1 Paul describes himself as an expert builder (*architectōn:* literally an architect). He recognizes that others will build on the foundation. How might this have influenced what Paul did, did not do, and for how long?

9.2 Do you have a clear sense of your ministry parameters? If not, what might it take for you to clarify your understanding?

A Case Study

Joel and his wife, Gabriella, are cross-cultural missionaries who have recently moved to a city in the country adjacent to their own. There is no Navigator ministry in the city. After a year of adjustment and meeting many people from all walks of life, Joel and Gabriella feel as if very little has happened. They are feeling discouraged and confused. They know that something needs to change, but they have no idea what.

A veteran missionary asked them several penetrating questions, such as, "What are you trusting God to do? How will this affect what you focus on?

How will you know when your contribution has ended?

Reflect on the scripture we just studied and The Four Contributions. How would you respond to the questions above? What might you do ahead of time to avoid the confusion faced by Joel and Gabriella?

EMERGING NAVIGATOR DIRECTIONS

The Navigator Core conveys the biblical foundation for our unique calling. Based on that solid ground, many Navigators around the world are seeing new ways to express The Core in light of changing cultural contexts. Noticing major themes in the Scriptures in fresh ways, they have sensed God leading them into ways of serving that did not previously play a prominent role in our history. These new ministry directions are emerging in response to God's leadership and his call to meet needs in a changing world.

This in no way means that other long-standing Navigator ministry approaches are outdated or less valuable. To the contrary, God continues to bless the work of Navigators who are laboring in ways that have a long and fruitful history. But a basic awareness of these more recent developments can help you think about your own ministry focus.

The three topics covered in this section are: the concept of missional enterprises, funding missions, and working among the poor and oppressed.

THE GOSPEL AMONG THE POOR AND OPPRESSED

Regardless of where we work, we will encounter the poor and oppressed. Therefore, it is crucial for our work to be shaped less by our preferences and more by the Word and the Spirit. Our Vision speaks of Gospel movements characterized by "a heart for the whole person and compassion for the vulnerable." It describes communities that are "bringing joy and hope to their surrounding environments as relationships are healed and justice increases."

Study 10: God's Heart for the Poor and Oppressed

EXODUS 3:7-10

The Lord said, "I have indeed seen the misery of my people in Egypt. I have heard them crying out because of their slave drivers, and I am concerned about their suffering. So I have come down to rescue them from the hand of the Egyptians and to bring them up out of that land into a good and spacious land, a land flowing with milk and honey—the home of the Canaanites, Hittites, Amorites, Perizzites, Hivites and Jebusites. And now the cry of the Israelites has reached me, and I have seen the way the Egyptians are oppressing them. So now, go. I am sending you to Pharaoh to bring my people the Israelites out of Egypt."

ISAIAH 58:6-7

Is not this the kind of fasting I have chosen: to loose the chains of injustice and untie the cords of the yoke, to set the oppressed free and break every yoke? Is it not to share your food with the hungry and to provide the poor wanderer with shelter—when you see the naked, to clothe them, and not to turn away from your own flesh and blood?

MATTHEW 25:34-36

Then the King will say to those on his right, 'Come, you who are blessed by my Father; take your inheritance, the kingdom prepared for you since the creation of the world. For I was hungry and you gave me something to eat, I was thirsty and you gave me something to drink, I was a stranger and you invited me in, I needed clothes and you clothed me, I was sick and you looked after me, I was in prison and you came to visit me.'

ACTS 4:13

When they saw the courage of Peter and John and realized that they were un-schooled, ordinary men, they were astonished and they took note that these men had been with Jesus.

1 CORINTHIANS 1:26-28

Brothers and sisters, think of what you were when you were called. Not many of you were wise by human standards; not many were influential; not many were of noble birth. But God chose the foolish things of the world to shame the wise; God chose the weak things of the world to shame the strong. God chose the lowly things of this world and the despised things—and the things that are not—to nullify the things that are . . .

2 CORINTHIANS 8:1-2

And now, brothers and sisters, we want you to know about the grace that God has given the Macedonian churches. In the midst of a very severe trial, their overflowing joy and their extreme poverty welled up in rich generosity.

GALATIANS 2:10

All they asked was that we should continue to remember the poor, the very thing I was eager to do.

Discover More

Download an excellent Navigator study titled *Responding to Poverty, Corruption and Injustice* by visiting www.navigatorsworldwide.org.

Think Deeper

10.1 According to Isaiah 58:6, how does God measure success for his servants, especially regarding our response to the poor and oppressed?

10.2 What did it look like as the early church introduced the Gospel into the lives of the poor and oppressed? What kinds of people are included in foundational generations?

Missional Enterprises

For our purposes, a missional enterprise is a legitimate business that exists to advance God's kingdom while being financially self-sustaining and adding value to the community.

God has always been working through businesses and commerce to advance his purposes. In the Scriptures, we see God's people involved in many types of commercial ventures, including agri-business, construction, trading, administration, micro-enterprise, manufacturing, and wealth management. God accomplished his work through these enterprises in remarkable ways.

We see that Jesus participated in the family carpentry business and that some of his closest friends and disciples were immersed in the fishing industry. Paul provides us with a clear view of how an enterprise, such as his low-cost housing business (making tents), could expand the kingdom.

Study 11: New Testament Perspectives on Missional Enterprises

Acts 18:1-3

After this, Paul left Athens and went to Corinth. There he met a Jew named Aquila, a native of Pontus, who had recently come from Italy with his wife Priscilla, because Claudius had ordered all Jews to leave Rome. Paul went to see them, and because he was a tentmaker as they were, he stayed and worked with them.

Acts 20:32-35

Now I commit you to God and to the word of his grace, which can build you up and give you an inheritance among all those who are sanctified. I have not coveted anyone's silver or gold or clothing. You yourselves know that these hands of mine have supplied my own needs and the needs of my companions. In everything I did, I showed you that by this kind of hard work we must help the weak, remembering the words the Lord Jesus himself said: 'It is more blessed to give than to receive.'

2 Thessalonians 3:8-9

. . . nor did we eat anyone's food without paying for it. On the contrary, we worked night and day, laboring and toiling so that we would not be a burden to any of you. We did this, not because we do not have the right to such help, but in order to offer ourselves as a model for you to imitate.

Discover More

Read about Paul's attitude toward his work: Titus 3:14; 2 Corinthians 6:3-5; 2 Corinthians 11:7-11; 2 Corinthians 12:13-18; 1 Thessalonians 2:9-10.

Think Deeper

11.1 How did Paul's tent business fit the definition of a missional enterprise?

11.2 How might a missional enterprise "make the teaching about God our Savior attractive" (Titus 2:10)?

11.3 In what ways could an enterprise contribute to the credibility, sustainability, and mobility of the Gospel in your cultural context? What might be some limitations of a missional enterprise?

Conventional Income and Gift Income

Historically, our Navigator Calling has been fulfilled around the world by people who are funded through generous gifts from a team of friends, and by people who serve Christ as they work in their professions. Both are important.

A healthy Navigator ministry is one in which ordinary people living ordinary lives are having an extraordinary impact in their communities. These people permeate the society as salt and light so that people can experience Jesus.

In addition, our international work requires some "gift-income people" who are free to devote full energy to specific ministry needs. If we are to have a movement of the Gospel across generations, the vision needs to be pursued by both types of people.

Study 12: Advancing the Gospel, All Walks of Life

Luke 8:3 (about Jesus and his team)

Joanna the wife of Chuza, the manager of Herod's household; Susanna; and many others. These women were helping to support them out of their own means.

Acts 11:20-26

Some of them, however, men from Cyprus and Cyrene, went to Antioch and began to speak to Greeks also, telling them the good news about the Lord Jesus. The Lord's hand was with them, and a great number of people believed and turned to the Lord. News of this reached the church in Jerusalem, and they sent Barnabas to Antioch. When he arrived and saw what the grace of God had done, he was glad and encouraged them all to remain true to the Lord with all their hearts. He was a good man, full of the Holy Spirit and faith, and a great number of people were brought to the Lord. Then Barnabas went to Tarsus to look for Saul, and when he found him, he brought him to Antioch. So for a whole year Barnabas and Saul met with the church and taught great numbers of people.

Acts 18:1-4

After this, Paul left Athens and went to Corinth. There he met a Jew named

Aquila, a native of Pontus, who had recently come from Italy with his wife Priscilla, because Claudius had ordered all Jews to leave Rome. Paul went to see them, and because he was a tentmaker as they were, he stayed and worked with them.

Acts 19:9-10

But some of them became obstinate; they refused to believe and publicly maligned the Way. So Paul left them. He took the disciples with him and had discussions daily in the lecture hall of Tyrannus.

Titus 3:13-14

Do everything you can to help Zenas the lawyer and Apollos on their way and see that they have everything they need. Our people must learn to devote themselves to doing what is good, in order to provide for urgent needs and not live unproductive lives.

Romans 16:23

Gaius, whose hospitality I and the whole church here enjoy, sends you his greetings. Erastus, who is the city's director of public works, and our brother Quartus send you their greetings.

Think Deeper

12.1 How did ordinary people advance the Gospel? What roles did Paul and Barnabas play? What can we observe about the ways they funded the efforts?

12.2 In your context and calling, which approach to ministry and funding do you think would best help you serve God's purposes? Why?

SECTION 2

GOD'S MESSAGE AND MISSION

In this section we will look at the essence of the Gospel—the message we proclaim in life and word. We will study what the Scriptures reveal about how the Gospel in the first century took root in a culture and then spread geographically and generationally.

In the world you will soon call home, you will find beauty, mystery, wonder and awe. You will also find trouble, injustice, evil, and pain. As you wrestle to understand this new culture, you will ask yourself several compelling questions: Why are we here? What difference can we make? How can we be certain that we are approaching our work the best way? In answer to these questions, Jesus gives us certain hope and purpose (1 Corinthians 3:11).

Even on the best of days, a power lurks under the surface to corrupt, ruin, divide, and destroy. The Scriptures teach us that sin has entered the world (Romans 5:12). The power of sin has corrupted every aspect of life. It extends from our hearts to our families, communities, and organizations. It affects companies, governments, and the culture that surrounds us. Sin separates us from God (Isaiah 59:2). It is the sacrifice of Jesus on the cross that pays the penalty for our sin (Romans 3:23-26) and destroys the power of sin to dominate our lives (Romans 6:11). It is the resurrection that authenticates our faith and gives us eternal hope (1 Corinthians 15:17ff).

We also face Satan, who is described as the ruler of this world (2 Corinthians 4:4). Jesus declared that Satan is intent on stealing, killing, and destroying the world of those created in the image of God. Scripture declares that he has a dominion in the world of this age (1 John 5:19).

How can we invite people to find love, peace, joy, grace, truth, and justice in Jesus? The Gospel is not about *our* story; it's about *his* story. It's not only about an invitation to personal salvation, it's God's story for all of history. In this study we will explore:

- The meaning of the Gospel of Jesus and his kingdom
- Worldview: How to plant the Gospel in diverse cultural soils
- Contextualization and the danger of syncretism

KNOWING THE GOSPEL

The Gospel can be thought of as "a pool in which a child may wade and an elephant can swim." It is both simple and infinitely profound. We cannot reduce or simplify it, and we also can't fully grasp its power and majesty. The word "Gospel" comes originally from the word, *angelos* (a messenger) or *angelo* (to announce). In its earliest usage it refers to the reward a messenger received for bringing good news. Later it came to be associated with the good news itself. In its use in the first century AD, the word didn't only announce a new era or time of blessing, but actually brought it into reality. The Gospel appears even in the Old Testament.

THE GOSPEL AS GOOD NEWS

Study 13: The "Good News," the Old Testament, and Jesus

PSALM 96:2-3

Sing to the Lord, praise his name; proclaim his salvation day after day. Declare his glory among the nations, his marvelous deeds among all peoples.

ISAIAH 52:7

How beautiful on the mountains are the feet of those who bring good news, who proclaim peace, who bring good tidings, who proclaim salvation, who say to Zion, "Your God reigns!"

ISAIAH 61:1

The Spirit of the Sovereign Lord is on me, because the Lord has anointed me to proclaim good news to the poor. He has sent me to bind up the brokenhearted, to proclaim freedom for the captives, and release from darkness for the prisoners . . .

ROMANS 1:15-17

That is why I am so eager to preach the gospel also to you who are in Rome. For I am not ashamed of the gospel, because it is the power of God that brings salvation to everyone who believes: first to the Jew, then to the Gentile. For in the gospel the righteousness of God is revealed—a righteousness that is by faith from first to last, just as it is written: "The righteous will live by faith."

ROMANS 3:19-26

Now we know that whatever the law says, it says to those who are under the law, so that every mouth may be silenced and the whole world held accountable to God. Therefore no one will be declared righteous in God's sight by the works of the law; rather, through the law we become conscious of our sin.

But now apart from the law the righteousness of God has been made known, to which the Law and the Prophets testify. This righteousness is given through faith in Jesus Christ to all who believe. There is no difference between Jew and Gentile, for all have sinned and fall short of the glory of God, and all are justified freely by his grace through the redemption that came by Christ Jesus. God presented Christ as a sacrifice of atonement, through the shedding of his blood—to be received by faith. He did this to demonstrate his righteousness, because in his forbearance he had left the sins committed beforehand unpunished— he did it to demonstrate his righteousness at the present time, so as to be just and the one who justifies those who have faith in Jesus.

Think Deeper

13.1 How do these passages enrich our understanding of the Gospel?

13.2 What is the "good news" for the people you will serve?

The Gospel of Jesus

Study 14: "The Gospel that Displays the Glory of Christ"

Romans 1:1-4

Paul, a servant of Christ Jesus, called to be an apostle and set apart for the gospel of God—the gospel he promised beforehand through his prophets in the Holy Scriptures regarding his Son, who as to his earthly life was a descendant of David, and who through the Spirit of holiness was appointed the Son of God in power by his resurrection from the dead: Jesus Christ our Lord.

Matthew 10:7-8

As you go, proclaim this message: 'The kingdom of heaven has come near.' Heal the sick, raise the dead, cleanse those who have leprosy, drive out demons. Freely you have received; freely give.

Luke 10:8-9

When you enter a town and are welcomed, eat what is offered to you. Heal the sick who are there and tell them, 'The kingdom of God has come near to you.'

Acts 5:42

Day after day, in the temple courts and from house to house, they never stopped teaching and proclaiming the good news that Jesus is the Messiah.

Acts 17:18

A group of Epicurean and Stoic philosophers began to debate with him. Some of them asked, "What is this babbler trying to say?" Others remarked, "He seems to be advocating foreign gods." They said this because Paul was preaching the good news about Jesus and the resurrection.

1 CORINTHIANS 15:1-4

Now, brothers and sisters, I want to remind you of the gospel I preached to you, which you received and on which you have taken your stand. By this gospel you are saved, if you hold firmly to the word I preached to you. Otherwise, you have believed in vain. For what I received I passed on to you as of first importance: that Christ died for our sins according to the Scriptures, that he was buried, that he was raised on the third day according to the Scriptures . . .

GALATIANS 1:11-12

I want you to know, brothers and sisters, that the gospel I preached is not of human origin. I did not receive it from any man, nor was I taught it; rather, I received it by revelation from Jesus Christ.

EPHESIANS 3:6-8

This mystery is that through the gospel the Gentiles are heirs together with Israel, members together of one body, and sharers together in the promise in Christ Jesus. I became a servant of this gospel by the gift of God's grace given me through the working of his power. Although I am less than the least of all the Lord's people, this grace was given me: to preach to the Gentiles the boundless riches of Christ.

COLOSSIANS 1:13-23

For he has rescued us from the dominion of darkness and brought us into the kingdom of the Son he loves, in whom we have redemption, the forgiveness of sins.

The Son is the image of the invisible God, the firstborn over all creation. For in him all things were created: things in heaven and on earth, visible and invisible, whether thrones or powers or rulers or authorities; all things have been created through him and for him. He is before all things, and in him all things hold together. And he is the head of the body, the church; he is the beginning and the firstborn from among the dead, so that in everything he might have the supremacy. For God was pleased to have all his fullness dwell in him, and through him to reconcile to himself all things, whether things on earth or things in heaven, by making peace through his blood, shed on the cross.

Once you were alienated from God and were enemies in your minds because of your evil behavior. But now he has reconciled you by Christ's physical body through death to present you holy in his sight, without blemish and free from accusation— if you continue in your faith, established and firm, and do not move from the hope held out in the gospel. This is the gospel that you heard and that has been proclaimed to every creature under heaven, and of which I, Paul, have become a servant.

Discover More

Deepen your understanding about the nature of the Gospel by studying Matthew 1:21; Matthew 3:1-3; John 1:29; Matthew 4:17; Mark 1:14-15; Matthew 4:23; Matthew 9:35; Matthew 11:2-5; Matthew 24:14; Luke 4:18; John 14:6; Acts 1:3; Acts 2:14-36; Acts 4:12; Acts 28:30-31.

Think Deeper

14.1 As we can see, it is impossible to separate the message from Jesus. How would you convey this truth to people in your culture?

THE GOSPEL OF HIS KINGDOM

In 2001, when the words "kingdom of God" were written into the Navigator Core, our international leaders realized that the term was not fully understood. Still, there was a sense of safety because the term was biblical. The kingdom of God is not easily grasped and cannot be easily defined. Jesus preferred to describe it rather than define it. He made observations about the kingdom through his parables and teaching.

The kingdom of God is about the reign of God, which he delegated to Jesus until the appropriate time in God's plans. The authority of Jesus to rule over all creation is another quality of Jesus that makes him the greatest news for humanity. His sovereignty is at the heart of the kingdom. This does not mean that all things are currently in submission to him, but that he has the power and authority, and one day everything will be fully submitted to him.

Study 15: The Kingdom of Jesus in the Old Testament

PSALM 103:19

The Lord has established His throne in the heavens, and His sovereignty rules over all.

PSALM 2

Why do the nations conspire and the peoples plot in vain? The kings of the earth rise up and the rulers band together against the Lord and against his anointed, saying, "Let us break their chains and throw off their shackles."

The One enthroned in heaven laughs; the Lord scoffs at them. He rebukes them in his anger and terrifies them in his wrath, saying, "I have installed my king on Zion, my holy mountain."

I will proclaim the Lord's decree: He said to me, "You are my son; today I have become your father. Ask me, and I will make the nations your inheritance, the ends of the earth your possession. You will break them with a rod of iron; you will dash them to pieces like pottery." Therefore, you kings, be wise; be warned, you rulers of the earth. Serve the Lord with fear and celebrate his rule with trembling. Kiss his son, or he will be angry and your way will lead to your destruction for his wrath can flare up in a moment. Blessed are all who take refuge in him.

PSALM 110

The Lord says to my lord: "Sit at my right hand until I make your enemies a footstool for your feet." The Lord will extend your mighty scepter from Zion, saying, "Rule in the midst of your enemies!" Your troops will be willing on your day of battle. Arrayed in holy splendor, your young men will come to you like dew from the morning's womb. The Lord has sworn and will not change his mind: "You are a priest forever, in the order of Melchizedek."

The Lord is at your right hand; he will crush kings on the day of his wrath. He will judge the nations, heaping up the dead and crushing the rulers of the whole earth. He will drink from a brook along the way, and so he will lift his head high.

DANIEL 2:44-45

In the time of those kings, the God of heaven will set up a kingdom that will never be destroyed, nor will it be left to another people. It will crush all those kingdoms and bring them to an end, but it will itself endure forever. This is the meaning of the vision of the rock cut out of a mountain, but not by human hands—a rock that broke the iron, the bronze, the clay, the silver and the gold to pieces. "The great God has shown the king what will take place in the future. The dream is true and its interpretation is trustworthy."

DANIEL 7:13-14

In my vision at night I looked, and there before me was one like a son of man, coming with the clouds of heaven. He approached the Ancient of Days and was led into his presence. He was given authority, glory and sovereign power; all nations and peoples of every language worshiped him. His dominion is an everlasting dominion that will not pass away, and his kingdom is one that will never be destroyed.

1 CHRONICLES 17:10-14

I declare to you that the Lord will build a house for you: When your days are over and you go to be with your ancestors, I will raise up your offspring to succeed you, one of your own sons, and I will establish his kingdom. He is the one who will build a house for me, and I will establish his throne forever. I will be his father, and he will be my son. I will never take my love away from him, as I took it away from your predecessor. I will set him over my house and my kingdom forever; his throne will be established forever.

Think Deeper

15.1 How do these passages help you share Jesus and his rule with the lost?

THE TEACHINGS OF JESUS ABOUT THE KINGDOM

When Christ began his ministry after being baptized, the first thing he preached was, "Repent, for the kingdom of heaven is near" (Matthew 4:17).

He called for a complete, 180-degree turnaround (the meaning of "repent") in how we think and live. He proclaimed the existence of a different reality, an eternal kingdom not of this world. He called for loyalty to this kingdom.

Jesus taught about his kingdom by telling stories and asking questions. His parables, in particular, give clues regarding the nature of the kingdom. The lessons of the kingdom in these stories are at once simple and unfathomably deep. To understand them can be a lifelong exploration.

Take some time to reflect on the parable of the weeds, found in Matthew 13:24-30 and Matthew 13:36-43; and the parable of the growing seed, found in Mark 4:26-29. Then consider these questions:

- What are the main points of each parable?
- How do they help us understand the Gospel of his kingdom?
- How do they help us communicate the Gospel cross-culturally?
- Do any other parables help us communicate the Gospel?

Study 16: The Power and Love of the King

The work of Jesus on the cross destroys the kingdom of darkness. In the following verses, note how Jesus deals decisively with Satan and sin. When Jesus returns, the injustice of the nations will be destroyed.

COLOSSIANS 1:20
. . . and through him to reconcile to himself all things, whether things on earth or things in heaven, by making peace through his blood, shed on the cross.

HEBREWS 2:14
Since the children have flesh and blood, he too shared in their humanity so that by his death he might break the power of him who holds the power of death—that is, the devil . . .

Revelation 1:5-6

. . . and from Jesus Christ, who is the faithful witness, the firstborn from the dead, and the ruler of the kings of the earth. To him who loves us and has freed us from our sins by his blood, and has made us to be a kingdom and priests to serve his God and Father—to him be glory and power for ever and ever!

Discover More

For more about Jesus and his kingdom, read Philippians 2:5-11; Revelation 11:15; Revelation 19:11-16; 1 Corinthians 15:20-28; Revelation 21:1-5.

Think Deeper

16.1 How is salvation explained in this clash of kingdoms? As cross-cultural servants, how might we expect this conflict to impact our efforts?

Spiritual Warfare and the Kingdom

As we carry the Gospel forward, we need to develop a biblical framework from which we can exercise faith and action in dealing with spiritual opposition. This section is not an exhaustive study about this topic. But for now, we can look at some foundational truths.

Scripture does not explicitly state when angelic creatures appeared, but we know that they had been created by the time of the Fall (Genesis 3), and they might have been present when heaven and earth were created (Job 38:6-7).

We read of many different kinds of creatures in the heavenly realms: cherubim, seraphim, principalities, angels, archangels, etc. When God created the angels along with the rest of creation he said that it was all "very good" (Genesis 1:31). The angels were created good. But Satan, along with some of the angels "fell" from their original state and became enemies of God. As we can see, some angels were sent to hell and held there in darkness until judgment (2 Peter 2:4), while others were free to roam the earth doing Satan's bidding (Daniel 12:12; Jude 9).

Study 17: Opposition from Satan and Evil Angels

JUDE 6

And the angels who did not keep their positions of authority but abandoned their proper dwelling—these he has kept in darkness, bound with everlasting chains for judgment on the great Day.

2 PETER 2:4

For if God did not spare angels when they sinned, but sent them to hell, putting them in chains of darkness to be held for judgment . . .

REVELATION 12:1-9

A great sign appeared in heaven: a woman clothed with the sun, with the moon under her feet and a crown of twelve stars on her head. . . . Then another sign appeared in heaven: an enormous red dragon with seven heads and ten horns and seven crowns on its heads. . . . The dragon stood in front of the woman who was about to give birth, so that it might devour her child the moment he was born. She gave birth to a son, a male child, who "will rule all the nations with an iron scepter." And her child was snatched up to God and to his throne. . . . The great dragon was hurled down—that ancient serpent called the devil, or Satan, who leads the whole world astray. He was hurled to the earth and his angels with him.

JOB 1:6-12

One day the angels came to present themselves before the Lord, and Satan also came with them. The Lord said to Satan, "Where have you come from?"

Satan answered the Lord, "From roaming throughout the earth, going back and forth on it." Then the Lord said to Satan, "Have you considered my servant Job? There is no one on earth like him; he is blameless and upright . . ."

"Does Job fear God for nothing?" Satan replied. "Have you not put a hedge around him and his household and everything he has? You have blessed the work of his hands, so that his flocks and herds are spread throughout the land. But now stretch out your hand and strike everything he has, and he will surely curse you to your face."

The Lord said to Satan, "Very well, then, everything he has is in your power, but on the man himself do not lay a finger." Then Satan went out from the presence of the Lord. . . . (See also Job 2:3-7.)

Think Deeper

17.1 In your ministry context, how might these forms of opposition affect your life and work?

℞

Study 18: Spiritual Warfare and Satan's Deceptions

1 TIMOTHY 4:1

 The Spirit clearly says that in later times some will abandon the faith and follow deceiving spirits and things taught by demons.

2 CORINTHIANS 11:13-14

 For such people are false apostles, deceitful workers, masquerading as apostles of Christ. And no wonder, for Satan himself masquerades as an angel of light.

2 CORINTHIANS 4:3-4

 And even if our gospel is veiled, it is veiled to those who are perishing. The god of this age has blinded the minds of unbelievers, so that they cannot see the light of the gospel that displays the glory of Christ, who is the image of God.

Think Deeper

18.1 Have you seen evil deception occurring in your life and in the lives of others? How have you responded?

OUR AUTHORITY AND SECURITY IN JESUS

As we have seen, Satan (the "father of lies") often operates through deception. But numerous biblical accounts tell of direct encounters with demons. Jesus confronted them. In every case, Jesus had complete authority over them. (See Luke 9:37-45 as one example.) Thus, the death and resurrection of Jesus have given us a secure foundation as we encounter spiritual opposition.

Study 19: Our Position of Strength in Jesus

HEBREWS 2:14

Since the children have flesh and blood, he too shared in their humanity so that by his death he might break the power of him who holds the power of death—that is, the devil.

EPHESIANS 1:18-22

I pray that the eyes of your heart may be enlightened in order that you may know the hope to which he has called you, the riches of his glorious inheritance in his holy people, and his incomparably great power for us who believe. That power is the same as the mighty strength he exerted when he raised Christ from the dead and seated him at his right hand in the heavenly realms, far above all rule and authority, power and dominion, and every name that is invoked, not only in the present age but also in the one to come. And God placed all things under his feet and appointed him to be head over everything for the church . . .

MATTHEW 28:18

Then Jesus came to them and said, "All authority in heaven and on earth has been given to me."

REVELATION 12:11

They triumphed over him by the blood of the Lamb and by the word of their testimony; they did not love their lives so much as to shrink from death.

EPHESIANS 6:11-17

Put on the full armor of God, so that you can take your stand against the devil's schemes. For our struggle is not against flesh and blood, but against the rulers, against the authorities, against the powers of this dark world and against the spiritual forces of evil in the heavenly realms. Therefore, put on the full armor of God, so that when the day of evil comes, you may be able to stand your ground, and after you have done everything, to stand. Stand firm then, with the belt of truth buckled around your waist, with the breastplate of righteousness in place, and with your feet fitted with the readiness that comes from the gospel of peace. In addition to all this, take up the shield of faith, with which you can extinguish all the flaming arrows of the evil one. Take the helmet of salvation and the sword of the Spirit, which is the word of God.

JAMES 4:7

Submit yourselves, then, to God. Resist the devil, and he will flee from you.

Discover More

For more about spiritual warfare, read 1 John 5:18-19; Luke 9:37-45; Colossians 1:13; 2 Corinthians 10:3-5.

Think Deeper

19.1 What is needed for us to help people in the midst of spiritual warfare?

THE GOSPEL AND CULTURE

God delights in diversity. In Genesis 10, we see God establishing many ethnicities (nations). The diversity he created forces us out of our culturally conditioned comfort zones. As we establish Gospel foundations, the cultures in which we work allow us to see the beauty of the Gospel—like a diamond—

in ways that would not be visible from only one perspective. As we plant the good news in unfamiliar cultures, we move forward (Matthew 9:35-38) in the confidence that the nations are God's idea.

Laying Gospel foundations is like planting seeds in the soil of human hearts. So, how do we work with the soil and plant the good news so that the Gospel will grow?

Every culture is corrupted by sin, yet within every culture God has prepared hearts in which the Gospel will take root. He "has not left himself without testimony" (Acts 14:17). In this sense, the nations are his redemptive strategy (Acts 17:26-27). Every culture has elements that the Gospel affirms, and there are other aspects of each culture that, because of the Gospel, must be confronted and transformed.

UNDERSTANDING WORLDVIEW

People in all nations have a worldview, a way of seeing reality. Everyone tries to make sense of the world, to answer the big questions of life: Who am I? Why am I here? What happens when I die? The combination of these beliefs inevitably forms each person's worldview, the person's way of interpreting reality. Central beliefs influence each person's values, what he or she holds dear. These values influence our decisions, what we pursue in life. Ultimately, the decisions result in the outcomes of life (for better or worse).

As cross-cultural missionaries, we must be aware of three worldviews: our own, the culture's, and the kingdom's. We should ask two questions: First, how can the Gospel speak into our culture's mindset in ways that people can understand? Second, are we conveying the true, pure Gospel to people, or a Gospel mixed with our cultural biases?

Because the Gospel of Jesus and his kingdom is universal, it can have a greater impact when kept pure. Distortions in the Gospel reduce its ability to spread in a new culture. Yet we all have our own culture and worldview. Therefore, we must place our trust in "the God who gives life to the dead and calls things that are not as though they were" (Romans 4:17). We must ask the Spirit, as we reflect on the Word, to develop in us a biblical worldview, a deep way of seeing with "the eyes of our heart" (Ephesians 1:18).

This challenge is one more crucial reason for why we must remain deeply engaged with the Scriptures! The Word corrects our own biases and molds our worldview to fit the true Gospel. The Word helps us understand our own culture and the new cultures in which we work because God is the creator of the nations, and "in him all things hold together" (Colossians 1:17).

Developing a *biblical* worldview is foundational for Navigators. Why?

- Unless we plant the Gospel with sensitivity to how the Gospel is understood and articulated in each culture, we will not advance the Gospel "into the nations."
- Our work is not about "self-help" change. God wants us to be *spiritually transformed* by his power, the renewing of our minds, not conformed to the ways of the world (Romans 12:1-2; 2 Corinthians 10:5).

Although there are still people in the world who know nothing about Jesus, most people have heard something basic about him. So it is unlikely that we will get a "clean board" as we help people understand the Gospel. They will have formed opinions about religion, questions of life and death, guilt, good and evil, etc.—but from within their own cultural worldview. It is important for us to consider the distance between *our* starting point and *theirs*. Failure to do this will lead to frustration and misunderstanding as we communicate cross-culturally.

THE GOSPEL AND THE FIRST-CENTURY WORLDVIEW

In the New Testament, we see a new worldview breaking into first-century cultures. Notice below some examples for cross-cultural communication.

Study 20: Communicating Jesus among Diverse Worldviews

1 Corinthians 9:19-27

Though I am free and belong to no one, I have made myself a slave to everyone, to win as many as possible. To the Jews I became like a Jew, to win the Jews. To those under the law I became like one under the law (though I myself am not under the law), so as to win those under the law. To those not having the law I became like one not having the law (though I am not free from God's law but am under Christ's law), so as to win those not having the law. To the weak I became weak, to win the weak. I have become all things to all people so that by all possible means I might save some. I do all this for the sake of the gospel, that I may share in its blessings. Do you not know that in a race all the runners run, but only one gets the prize? Run in such a way as to get the prize. Everyone who competes in the games goes into strict training. They do it to get a crown that will not last, but we do it to get a crown that will last forever. Therefore, I do not run like someone running aimlessly; I do not fight like a boxer beating the air. No, I strike a blow to my body and make it my slave so that after I have preached to others, I myself will not be disqualified for the prize.

Colossians 4:2-5

Devote yourselves to prayer, being watchful and thankful. And pray for us, too, that God may open a door for our message, so that we may proclaim the mystery of Christ, for which I am in chains. Pray that I may proclaim it clearly, as I should. Be wise in the way you act toward outsiders; make the most of every opportunity.

Proverbs 18:13

To answer before listening—that is folly and shame.

Proverbs 20:5

The purposes of a person's heart are deep waters, but one who has insight draws them out.

1 Thessalonians 2:1-10

You know, brothers and sisters, that our visit to you was not without results. We had previously suffered and been treated outrageously in Philippi, as you know, but with the help of our God we dared to tell you his gospel in the face of strong opposition. For the appeal we make does not spring from error or impure motives, nor are we trying to trick you. On the contrary, we speak as those approved by God to be entrusted with the gospel. We are not trying to please people but God, who tests our hearts. You know we never used flattery, nor did we put on a mask to cover up greed—God is our witness. We were not looking for praise from people, not from you or anyone else, even though as apostles of Christ we could have asserted our authority. Instead, we were like young children among you. Just as a nursing mother cares for her children, so we cared for you. Because we loved you so much, we were delighted to share with you not only the gospel of God but our lives as well. Surely you remember, brothers and sisters, our toil and hardship; we worked night and day in order not to be a burden to anyone while we preached the gospel of God to you. You are witnesses, and so is God, of how holy, righteous and blameless we were among you who believed.

PHILIPPIANS 2:3-8

Do nothing out of selfish ambition or vain conceit. Rather, in humility value others above yourselves, not looking to your own interests but each of you to the interests of the others. In your relationships with one another, have the same mindset as Christ Jesus: Who, being in very nature God, did not consider equality with God something to be used to his own advantage; rather, he made himself nothing by taking the very nature of a servant, being made in human likeness. And being found in appearance as a man, he humbled himself by becoming obedient to death—even death on a cross!

Think Deeper

20.1 Jesus had supernatural insight into people and cultures; for us, it can require time, attentiveness, and learning. What can you learn from Jesus to help you understand cultures and worldviews different than your own?

A Case Study

Harriet has invested a lot of time in her friend Ana, a European. She has a good relationship with her, but she is frustrated by Ana's lack of responsiveness to the Gospel. Ana says things like: "How dare you say that I don't understand the Christian Gospel? Americans have no right to talk to us about Jesus. Give me a break! We've seen and lived through more Christianity on this continent than you'll ever understand."

Ana reminds Harriet that Christendom had dominated her region for centuries. She talks about how "Christians," in the name of Christ, brutally stamped out heresy, fought religious wars, went on bloody crusades, carried out book burnings and inquisitions, etc. "So wasn't all of that Christianity?" Ana blurted out. "Is that Christianity? If so, I want no part."

Harriet's message to Ana was being processed through Ana's worldview, her perception of reality. What steps would Harriet need to take to help Ana gain a clear understanding of the Gospel?

CONTEXTUALIZATION

As we cross cultures with the Gospel, we will face a crucial tension between two poles. Jesus captured this tension well when he prayed for his disciples to be "in the world" but not "of the world" (see John 17). This tension is often described by using two words: contextualization and syncretism.

Contextualization is, in a basic sense, the effort to communicate truth in ways that can be understood in a given culture—without distorting truth. Jesus came as a Jew, in human form, speaking local languages, and using stories to convey powerful truth. He was a master at contextualization! This is important for the Gospel to be understood, received, and passed to the next generations.

Syncretism is the mixing of multiple worldviews (cultural, religious, etc.).

It is like putting distinct ingredients into a blender and then turning it on. The distinct ingredients can no longer be identified. This happens with worldviews as people combine all sorts of ideas in their minds and hearts. While taking the Gospel into new cultures, we must not mix the Gospel with anything else.

Therein lies the tension and danger. If our attempt to contextualize the Gospel involves a conscious or unconscious blending of the pure Gospel with non-Gospel beliefs or practices, we will produce a distorted Gospel.

The Gospel is superior to all cultures and meaningful in all cultures. Therefore, it must remain pure as it crosses cultures. A pure Gospel is very mobile. The Gospel "becomes flesh" in the host culture as it is expressed in life and word through the faith (Romans 14:17) of believers.

The danger of syncretism should cause us to guard the purity of the Gospel on two fronts. First, missionaries must guard against adding their *own traditions* to the Gospel. E. Stanley Jones, missionary in India in the early twentieth century, in his book *Christ on the Indian Road,* said, "(Hindus) may have Jesus without the systems that have been built around him in the West." Second, we need to guard against allowing certain traditions and beliefs in the host culture to compromise the purity of the Gospel.

It takes discernment to know how to proceed in relationships with non-believers. Sometimes the boundaries are clear. A believer would not go into a striptease bar with non-believing friends in order to maintain relationships. And, in an animistic culture, one would not participate in certain demonic rituals so as to fit into the culture. Paul addresses this issue in 1 Corinthians 10.

"Consider the people of Israel: Do not those who eat the sacrifices participate in the altar? Do I mean then that food sacrificed to an idol is anything, or that an idol is anything? No, but the sacrifices of pagans are offered to demons, not to God, and I do not want you to be participants with demons. . . . If an unbeliever invites you to a meal and you want to go, eat whatever is put before you without raising questions of conscience. But if someone says to you, "This has been offered in sacrifice," then do not eat it, both for the sake of the one who told you and for the sake of conscience. I am referring to the other person's conscience, not yours. For why is my freedom being judged by another's conscience?"

But in other situations, the lines between healthy contextualization and syncretism are not so clear. We need humility and wisdom from God to carry the Gospel forward, to be "in the world" but not "of the world" as Jesus prayed in John 17. When we pass on an impure Gospel, we make it more difficult to build a multiplying ministry that results in spiritual generations.

AVOIDING SYNCRETISM
Study 21: Guarding a Pure Gospel

The New Testament gives us many examples of how Jesus and the apostles worked hard to preserve a pure Gospel as it spread cross-culturally. In Mark 7 (below) we see Jesus refuting Jewish leaders for allowing their religious traditions to become more important than the actual message of Christ and the purposes of God. Then, as the Gospel began to spread from its origins in a Jewish culture to multiple non-Jewish ethnic groups, the early believers had to learn how to advance the Gospel without requiring non-Jewish believers to adopt Jewish customs and teachings. At stake was the purity of the Gospel and its ability to advance through regions and into next generations. This struggle is documented primarily in Acts 15 and in Paul's letter to the Galatians.

MARK 7:1-13
The Pharisees and some of the teachers of the law who had come from Jerusalem gathered around Jesus and saw some of his disciples eating food with hands that were defiled, that is, unwashed. (The Pharisees and all the Jews do not eat unless

they give their hands a ceremonial washing, holding to the tradition of the elders. When they come from the marketplace they do not eat unless they wash. And they observe many other traditions, such as the washing of cups, pitchers and kettles.) So the Pharisees and teachers of the law asked Jesus, "Why don't your disciples live according to the tradition of the elders instead of eating their food with defiled hands?"

He replied, "Isaiah was right when he prophesied about you hypocrites; as it is written: "'These people honor me with their lips, but their hearts are far from me. They worship me in vain; their teachings are merely human rules.' You have let go of the commands of God and are holding on to human traditions."

And he continued, "You have a fine way of setting aside the commands of God in order to observe your own traditions! For Moses said, 'Honor your father and mother,' and, 'Anyone who curses their father or mother is to be put to death.' But you say that if anyone declares that what might have been used to help their father or mother is Corban (that is, devoted to God)— then you no longer let them do anything for their father or mother. Thus you nullify the word of God by your tradition that you have handed down. And you do many things like that."

ACTS 15:1, 5; 7-11, 19

Some men came down from Judea to Antioch and were teaching the brothers: "Unless you are circumcised, according to the custom taught by Moses, you cannot be saved. . . . Then some of the believers who belonged to the party of the Pharisees stood up and said, "The Gentiles must be circumcised and required to obey the law of Moses."

. . . After much discussion, Peter addressed them: "Brothers, you know that some time ago God made a choice among you that the Gentiles might hear from my lips the message of the gospel and believe. God, who knows the heart, showed that he accepted them by giving the Holy Spirit to them, just as he did to us. He made no distinction between us and them, for he purified their hearts by faith. Now then, why do you try to test God by putting on the necks of the disciples a yoke that neither we nor our fathers have been able to bear? No! We believe it is through the grace of our Lord Jesus that we are saved, just as they are. . . . It is my judgment, therefore, that we should not make it difficult for the Gentiles who are turning to God.

GALATIANS 1:6-8 (PAUL, WRITING TO GENTILES)

I am astonished that you are so quickly deserting the one who called you by the grace of Christ and are turning to a different gospel, which is really no gospel at all. Evidently some people are throwing you into confusion and are trying to pervert the gospel of Christ.

Galatians 1:11-12

I want you to know, brothers, that the gospel I preached is not something that man made up. I did not receive it from any man, nor was I taught it; rather, I received it by revelation from Jesus Christ.

Galatians 2:4-5

This matter arose because some false brothers had infiltrated our ranks to spy on the freedom we have in Christ Jesus and to make us slaves. We did not give in to them for a moment, so that the truth of the gospel might remain with you.

Galatians 2:14-16

When I saw that they (Jewish believers, such as Peter) were not acting in line with the truth of the gospel, I said to Peter in front of them all, "You are a Jew, yet you live like a Gentile and not like a Jew. How is it, then, that you force Gentiles to follow Jewish customs? We who are Jews by birth and not 'Gentile sinners' know that a man is not justified by observing the law, but by faith in Jesus Christ. So we, too, have put our faith in Christ Jesus that we may be justified by faith in Christ and not by observing the law, because by observing the law no one will be justified."

Galatians 5:1-2, 4-6

It is for freedom that Christ has set you free. Stand firm, then, and do not let yourselves be burdened again by a yoke of slavery. Mark my words! I, Paul, tell you that if you let yourselves be circumcised, Christ will be of no value to you at all. . . . You who are trying to be justified by law have been alienated from Christ; you have fallen away from grace. But by faith we eagerly await through the Spirit the righteousness for which we hope. For in Christ Jesus neither circumcision nor uncircumcision has any value. The only thing that counts is faith expressing itself through love.

Discover More

To observe how Jesus interacted with his surrounding culture, read John 4:1-42; Mark 5:1-20; Matthew 15:21-28; Galatians 1:11-24; Philippians 3:1-10. Study more about the pure Gospel in relation to freedom, conscience and judgment in these passages: Romans 14:1-15:7; 1 Corinthians 8:1-13; 1 Corinthians 10:14-22 and 23-33.

Think Deeper

21.1 Based on Galatians, what do we learn about protecting the purity of the Gospel? What was the theological impurity that Paul sought to correct?

21.2 In Acts 15, everyone agreed to let the Gospel advance among the gentile ethnicities without imposing Jewish customs on them. What might have happened if everyone hadn't reached this conclusion?

A Case Study

Jeremiah (not his real name) is a mobile leader with a supervisory role over a ministry in the country of Faraway. The people of Faraway were never colonized by foreigners. For centuries they lived under an ancient monarchy. Special land rights and class privileges were given to priests, soldiers, and civil servants. The other subjects were bound to servitude. Still today, the class a person is born into determines his or her status in society. Class divisions and legalism were, over the centuries, attached to the Gospel.

More recently, evangelical missionaries have entered the country. Some have worked among poorer classes while others have served among wealthy classes. Divisions between the believers in each economic class have emerged.

Jeremiah's attempts to integrate, inspire, and equip believers to advance the Gospel through families and relational networks have met little success. The leaders of the ministry mistrust Jeremiah and he's fearful that anything he does will antagonize one group or the other.

Looking at the history of Faraway, what deficiencies affected the ability of a pure Gospel to advance in the culture? What advice would you give Jeremiah? What can he do now to promote a better scenario for future generations?

LAYING GOSPEL FOUNDATIONS

People don't need our culture; they need Jesus. This truth should condition the ways in which we do our work. We can either view culture as an obstacle to our mission, or we can view it as a vehicle that can serve the Gospel, helping to carry it forward.

A Crucial First-Century Struggle

The New Testament account of the first-century movement of the Gospel from its Jewish roots into the gentile nations is the ultimate case study in contextualization. Jesus focused on the Jewish people and culture. From there, the church was birthed within the Jewish culture, a community that had experienced sixteen centuries of planting and cultivating via the patriarchs, prophets, priests, and kings.

As we saw earlier, Acts 15 records a pivotal event. It's the account of the conflict over the role of the Mosaic laws for followers of Christ. Paul and Barnabas held that those laws no longer applied. Others insisted that "the

Gentiles must be circumcised and obey the laws of Moses" (verse 5). Imagine that you had grown up reading Moses' writings, that you had memorized Genesis 17:12-14. Which side of this debate would you have been on?

The pure Gospel says that faith in Christ is all that is needed for salvation and everything else in life. By holding fast to this truth, Paul was laying solid foundations for spiritual generations. If the Gospel message had been distorted in the beginning, the rest of the building would be distorted.

The first-century solution? Paul wrote in Galatians 5:1 that Christ has set us free from a mandate to follow specific religious forms and traditions. We are free to focus on Jesus alone and the pure Gospel, with nothing else attached. The New Testament also gives us some universal principles for cross-cultural movements of the Gospel.

HOW THE GOSPEL SPREADS

Study 22: Factors for Expansion

1 THESSALONIANS 1:5-9

. . . because our gospel came to you not simply with words but also with power, with the Holy Spirit and deep conviction. You know how we lived among you for your sake. You became imitators of us and of the Lord, for you welcomed the message in the midst of severe suffering with the joy given by the Holy Spirit. And so you became a model to all the believers in Macedonia and Achaia. The Lord's message rang out from you not only in Macedonia and Achaia—your faith in God has become known everywhere. Therefore, we do not need to say anything about it, for they themselves report what kind of reception you gave us. They tell how you turned to God from idols to serve the living and true God . . .

PHILIPPIANS 2:14-16

Do everything without grumbling or arguing, so that you may become blameless and pure, "children of God without fault in a warped and crooked generation." Then you will shine among them like stars in the sky as you hold firmly to the word of life. And then I will be able to boast on the day of Christ that I did not run or labor in vain.

Ephesians 5: 8-16

For you were once darkness, but now you are light in the Lord. Live as children of light (for the fruit of the light consists in all goodness, righteousness and truth) and find out what pleases the Lord. Have nothing to do with the fruitless deeds of darkness, but rather expose them. It is shameful even to mention what the disobedient do in secret. But everything exposed by the light becomes visible—and everything that is illuminated becomes a light. This is why it is said: "Wake up, sleeper, rise from the dead, and Christ will shine on you." Be very careful, then, how you live—not as unwise but as wise, making the most of every opportunity, because the days are evil.

Colossians 4:2-6

Devote yourselves to prayer, being watchful and thankful. And pray for us, too, that God may open a door for our message, so that we may proclaim the mystery of Christ, for which I am in chains. Pray that I may proclaim it clearly, as I should. Be wise in the way you act toward outsiders; make the most of every opportunity. Let your conversation be always full of grace, seasoned with salt, so that you may know how to answer everyone.

John 17:13-23

I am coming to you now, but I say these things while I am still in the world, so that they may have the full measure of my joy within them. I have given them your word and the world has hated them, for they are not of the world any more than I am of the world. My prayer is not that you take them out of the world but that you protect them from the evil one. They are not of the world, even as I am not of it. Sanctify them by the truth; your word is truth. As you sent me into the world, I have sent them into the world. For them I sanctify myself, that they too may be truly sanctified. My prayer is not for them alone. I pray also for those who will believe in me through their message, that all of them may be one, Father, just as you are in me and I am in you. May they also be in us so that the world may believe that you have sent me. I have given them the glory that you gave me, that they may be one as we are one—I in them and you in me—so that they may be brought to complete unity. Then the world will know that you sent me and have loved them even as you have loved me.

Think Deeper

22.1 How will these scriptures affect your approach to ministry?

THE GOSPEL SPREADING THROUGH HOUSEHOLDS

As the church expanded beyond Judaism and into the Greco-Roman world, the household (*oikos*) was a primary vehicle for the Gospel's mobility. A household in that era was the basic unit of the society. It was an integrated system that included the family, education, work, trade, leisure, and religion.

The first-century churches did not invent many new forms. Instead, they used the existing social structure, the household and relational networks, as the basic vehicle. The message tended to flow within a household, and then from household to household—reaching the whole social spectrum.

Study 23: Households and Relational Networks

ACTS 16:13-15

On the Sabbath we went outside the city gate to the river, where we expected to find a place of prayer. We sat down and began to speak to the women who had gathered there. One of those listening was a woman from the city of Thyatira named Lydia, a dealer in purple cloth. She was a worshiper of God. The Lord opened her heart to respond to Paul's message. When she and the members of her household were baptized, she invited us to her home. "If you consider me a believer in the Lord," she said, "come and stay at my house." And she persuaded us.

ROMANS 16:5-6

Greet also the church that meets at their house. Greet my dear friend Epenetus, who was the first convert to Christ in the province of Asia. Greet Mary, who worked very hard for you.

1 CORINTHIANS 16:15-19

You know that the household of Stephanas were the first converts in Achaia, and they have devoted themselves to the service of the Lord's people. I urge you, brothers and sisters, to submit to such people and to everyone who joins in the work and labors at it. I was glad when Stephanas, Fortunatus and Achaicus arrived, because they have supplied what was lacking from you. . . . The churches in the province of Asia send you greetings. Aquila and Priscilla greet you warmly in the Lord, and so does the church that meets at their house.

1 TIMOTHY 3:4-5

He must manage his own family well and see that his children obey him, and he must do so in a manner worthy of full respect. (If anyone does not know how to manage his own family, how can he take care of God's church?)

Think Deeper

23.1 We can't return to the first century, but there are principles from that time that can help us advance the Gospel. What can instruct us today?

A VISION FOR SPIRITUAL GENERATIONS

We are called to help the Gospel penetrate nations and cultures, and to advance the Gospel through "spiritual generations of laborers living and discipling among the lost." Our Navigator Vision, shown below, paints a picture of how this should look.

> We see a vital movement of the Gospel, fueled by prevailing prayer, flowing freely through relational networks and out into the nations. Workers for the kingdom are next door to every-

where! Ordinary people, in many walks of life, are joyfully leading integrated lives. They live as fruitful insiders among the lost. . . . Around the world, many are coming to faith. As they become established in discipleship, some grow to be foundational for further generations. The Gospel spreads naturally and powerfully, as believers share Christ life upon life, family to family.

Study 24: Portraits of God's Generational Work

DEUTERONOMY 6:1-9

These are the commands, decrees and laws the Lord your God directed me to teach you to observe in the land that you are crossing the Jordan to possess, so that you, your children and their children after them may fear the Lord your God as long as you live by keeping all his decrees and commands that I give you, and so that you may enjoy long life. . . . Impress them on your children. Talk about them when you sit at home and when you walk along the road, when you lie down and when you get up. Tie them as symbols on your hands and bind them on your foreheads. Write them on the door frames of your houses and on your gates.

JOHN 17:20

My prayer is not for them alone. I pray also for those who will believe in me through their message . . .

ROMANS 4:13-17

It was not through the law that Abraham and his offspring received the promise that he would be heir of the world, but through the righteousness that comes by faith. For if those who depend on the law are heirs, faith means nothing and the promise is worthless, because the law brings wrath. And where there is no law there is no transgression. Therefore, the promise comes by faith, so that it may be by grace and may be guaranteed to all Abraham's offspring—not only to those who are of the law but also to those who have the faith of Abraham. . . . As it is written: "I have made you a father of many nations." He is our father in the sight of God, in whom he believed—the God who gives life to the dead and calls into being things that were not.

2 TIMOTHY 2:2

And the things you have heard me say in the presence of many witnesses entrust to reliable people who will also be qualified to teach others.

Think Deeper

24.1 In what ways can you work to produce spiritual generations? What are your limitations? What is God's role?

A Case Study

In a developing country's capital city, Navigator pioneers are laying foundations for spiritual generations in different neighborhoods. One group is making Christ known through a shop that employs deaf women. Another group is making Christ known through a service for refugees. Another is making Christ known through a fitness gym where upper-class nationals exercise together. All three are bearing fruit. If you were launching a Navigator ministry in a similar setting, how might you decide which socio-economic sector of the city to focus on? How might the Scriptures shape your decision?

A Case Study

Graduates of a new Navigator university ministry in Africa were studying the Bible together when one said she felt drawn to help prostitutes. Her family was opposed, and the others in the study were reluctant. How might the Scriptures you've studied influence the response of this discipleship group? What might be some positive and negative consequences of encouraging this young woman to proceed?

GOD'S PEOPLE AND DISCIPLESHIP

We can't grow in Christ by ourselves, and the Gospel can't spread without a collective effort. So, in this section, we will look closely at the nature and essence of *ekklesia*, or church.

The first part of this section is about the biblical basis for our freedom to develop local expressions of the church that are culturally relevant and biblically sound. This will help the Gospel to move forward through relational networks and help people to become Christlike.

The IET has produced a more extensive study on *ekklesia*. We encourage you to download it from the resource library of the International Leadership Community site (www.ilcworldwide.org) or by contacting your leader/mentor.

EKKLESIA: WHAT IS CHURCH?

How are people transformed? How can the Gospel move through natural relational networks? We cannot do either of these alone. We need "safe" communities where we can address life issues and experience spiritual transformation. By "safe" we mean relationships in which people find grace and forgiveness while at the same time being admonished to grow in holiness and sanctification. Jesus treated the woman caught in adultery with grace, telling her, "Then neither do I condemn you." But he also commanded her to leave her life of sin (see John 8:10-11). A "safe community" does not accommodate sin; rather, the community encourages people in the grace and love of God to confess their sins to one another so that they can escape the bondage of sin (see 1 John 1). We are called to be holy, which is essential for our well-being and so that we can represent Christ in the world. As 1 Peter 2:12 says, "Live such good lives among the pagans that, though they accuse you of doing wrong, they may see your good deeds and glorify God on the day he visits us."

Our long-term goal is to see followers of Christ in communities that labor together as fruitful insiders, people who have a generational impact. The New Testament refers to such communities using the Greek word *ekklesia*, which is generally translated in English as "church." The word comes from two root meanings: *ek*, "out of," and *klesis*, "a calling" (*kaleo*, to call).

In the Greco-Roman world, *ekklesia* was also used for an assembly called to discuss public issues. *Ekklesia* was, in this example, a political gathering (e.g. Acts 19:32, 39). The term was also used by Jesus and the apostles to describe the people of God called to himself. Just as the Roman world called people out of their homes and summoned them to an assembly, Jesus calls us to be distinct from the world and summons us to himself.

What we understand about *ekklesia* and how it is expressed in different cultures is of crucial importance if we are to see the Gospel progress among people who are different than us. Biblical clarity about *ekklesia* gives us the freedom to affirm local expressions of church in different ethnic, cultural, and religious contexts.

What is *ekklesia*? What are the biblical essentials of *ekklesia*? What might church look like in the culture where you will serve?

Study 25: The Term "Church" in the Four Gospels

Matthew 16:18

And I tell you that you are Peter, and on this rock I will build my church, and the gates of Hades will not overcome it.

Matthew 18:15-17

If your brother or sister sins, go and point out their fault, just between the two of you. If they listen to you, you have won them over. But if they will not listen, take one or two others along, so that 'every matter may be established by the testimony of two or three witnesses.' If they still refuse to listen, tell it to the church; and if they refuse to listen even to the church, treat them as you would a pagan or a tax collector.

Think Deeper

25.1 The references from Matthew above are the only two places in the four Gospels that use the word "church." How do you think Jesus's disciples would have understood this word?

THE GOSPEL AND THE PEOPLE OF GOD

Study 26: Our Identity as God's People

EPHESIANS 1:1-14

Praise be to the God and Father of our Lord Jesus Christ, who has blessed us in the heavenly realms with every spiritual blessing in Christ. For he chose us in him before the creation of the world to be holy and blameless in his sight. In love he predestined us for adoption to sonship through Jesus Christ, in accordance with his pleasure and will—to the praise of his glorious grace, which he has freely given us in the One he loves. In him we have redemption through his blood, the forgiveness of sins, in accordance with the riches of God's grace that he lavished on us. With all wisdom and understanding, he made known to us the mystery of his will according to his good pleasure, which he purposed in Christ, to be put into effect when the times reach their fulfillment—to bring unity to all things in heaven and on earth under Christ.

In him we were also chosen, having been predestined according to the plan of him who works out everything in conformity with the purpose of his will, in order that we, who were the first to put our hope in Christ, might be for the praise of his glory. And you also were included in Christ when you heard the message of truth, the gospel of your salvation. When you believed, you were marked in him with a seal, the promised Holy Spirit, who is a deposit guaranteeing our inheritance until the redemption of those who are God's possession—to the praise of his glory.

JOHN 1:10-12

He was in the world, and though the world was made through him, the world did not recognize him. He came to that which was his own, but his own did not receive him. Yet to all who did receive him, to those who believed in his name, he gave the right to become children of God . . .

ROMANS 9:22-26

What if God, although choosing to show his wrath and make his power known, bore with great patience the objects of his wrath—prepared for destruction? What if he did this to make the riches of his glory known to the objects of his mercy, whom he prepared in advance for glory—even us, whom he also called, not only from the Jews but also from the Gentiles? As he says in Hosea: "I will call them 'my people' who are not my people; and I will call her 'my loved one' who is not my loved one," and, "In the very place where it was said to them, 'You are not my people,' there they will be called 'children of the living God.'"

Think Deeper

26.1 What is each believer's primary identity, and the foundation of that identity? How does identity in Christ enable us to effectively cross-cultures?

BELONGING TO GOD AND TO ONE ANOTHER

The need to belong to a community runs deep in every human heart. For people in some cultures, there is a tendency to define oneself by this temple or that church. In other cultures, people seek to establish identity through achievements, work, fame, or wealth. Still others seek identity by gaining acceptance into a group of friends. The Scriptures offer more hope.

Study 27: The Believer's True Identity

COLOSSIANS 3:11-12

Here there is no Greek or Jew, circumcised or uncircumcised, barbarian, Scythian, slave or free, but Christ is all, and is in all. Therefore, as God's chosen people, holy and dearly loved, clothe yourselves with compassion, kindness, humility, gentleness and patience.

1 PETER 2:9-10

But you are a chosen people, a royal priesthood, a holy nation, God's special possession, that you may declare the praises of him who called you out of darkness into his wonderful light. Once you were not a people, but now you are the people of God; once you had not received mercy, but now you have received mercy.

EPHESIANS 2:19-22

Consequently, you are no longer foreigners and strangers, but fellow citizens with God's people and also members of his household, built on the foundation of the apostles and prophets, with Christ Jesus himself as the chief cornerstone. In him the whole building is joined together and rises to become a holy temple in the Lord. And in him you too are being built together to become a dwelling in which God lives by his Spirit.

1 CORINTHIANS 12:13

For we were all baptized by one Spirit so as to form one body—whether Jews or Gentiles, slave or free—and we were all given the one Spirit to drink.

EPHESIANS 1:22-23

And God placed all things under his feet and appointing him to be head over everything for the church, which is his body, the fullness of him who fills everything in every way.

Think Deeper

27.1 Summarize the essential qualities of a biblical *ekklesia*?

27.2 What other metaphors are used in the Scriptures to describe the "people of God"? What terms for *ekklesia* would work well in the culture where you are or will be serving?

27.3 Many people understand identity in communal and visual terms, often using rituals and symbols. Gang members wear colors and tattoos. Hindus mark their foreheads and participate in festivals. Muslims say the Shahada. Most Christians experience baptism, the Lord's Supper, and physical meetings as communal identity markers. What identity markers may or may not be helpful for followers of Christ in your cross-cultural context?

THE RELATIONAL NATURE OF EKKLESIA

God's heart and mission are essentially about us being one with him and one with each other (John 17). Likewise, our mission is relational. Jesus modeled relational principles that we can imitate. By imitating him, we can relate well with one another and glorify him among the lost.

Integrity: The word "integrity" describes a character that is pure and un-mixed, righteous and holy. Jesus never deviated from God's righteousness. We are called to live the same way, as you can see in Ephesians 4:20-25.

> That, however, is not the way of life you learned when you heard about Christ and were taught in him in accordance with the truth that is in Jesus. You were taught, with regard to your former way of life, to put off your old self, which is being corrupted by its deceitful desires; to be made new in the attitude of your minds; and to put on the new self, created to be like God in true righteousness and holiness. Therefore, each of you must put off falsehood and speak truthfully to your neighbor, for we are all members of one body.

Love: Although we try, we lack integrity. If God dealt with us only on the basis of his righteous and holy standard, we would not survive. Romans 3:23 says that we all fall short of God's perfect law. Thankfully, God loves us. The apostle John stated that, "This how we know what love is: Christ died for us." Jesus is the full embodiment of love, as we read in Ephesians 5:1-2.

> Follow God's example, therefore, as dearly loved children and walk in the way of love, just as Christ loved us and gave himself up for us as a fragrant offering and sacrifice to God.

Based on the scripture above, and based on other passages about the love of Jesus, how would you define love? What does love look like in action?

Humility: It is phenomenal that the Lord of the universe, the creator of all things, could also be called humble. It is hard not to be deeply moved by what we read about Jesus in Philippians 2:3-8.

> Do nothing out of selfish ambition or vain conceit. Rather, in humility value others above yourselves, not looking to your own interests but each of you to the interests of the others. In your relationships

> with one another, have the same mindset as Christ Jesus: Who, being in very nature God, did not consider equality with God something to be used to his own advantage; rather, he made himself nothing by taking the very nature of a servant, being made in human likeness. And being found in appearance as a man, he humbled himself by becoming obedient to death—even death on a cross!

Jesus was humble, but not weak. What is humility's power in relationships?

Forgiveness: If we're honest, forgiveness seems terribly unfair. It's the last thing that someone who has been offended or hurt wants to do. Yet Jesus commanded his people to forgive one another. Read Matthew 18:23-35 to gain a deeper understanding of forgiveness. Ephesians 4:31-32, shown below, also demonstrates how Jesus embodied forgiveness.

> Get rid of all bitterness, rage and anger, brawling and slander, along with every form of malice. Be kind and compassionate to one another, forgiving each other, just as in Christ God forgave you.

What does the story Jesus told in Matthew 18 tell us about forgiveness and why it is so difficult to forgive? What happens to relationships and people when there is no forgiveness?

The "One Another" Nature of Ekklesia

Scripture often shows the phrases "one another" and "each other" being used to encourage the early churches to develop relational strength.

Study 28: Healthy Relational Dynamics

John 13:34

A new command I give you: Love one another. As I have loved you, so you must love one another.

ROMANS 12:10

Be devoted to one another in love. Honor one another above yourselves.

ROMANS 14:13

Therefore, let us stop passing judgment on one another.

2 CORINTHIANS 13:11

Finally, brothers and sisters, rejoice! Strive for full restoration, encourage one another, be of one mind, live in peace. . . .

I JOHN 4:12

No one has ever seen God; but if we love one another, God lives in us and his love is made complete in us.

Think Deeper

28.1 Why do you think these relational qualities are so prominent in the New Testament? How should they be expressed in *ekklesia*?

EKKLESIA AMONG THE LOST

The relational heart of God, his ongoing pursuit to gather people to himself, tells us a lot about the essence of biblical church. We need one another to become mature and to live healthy lives. But the church is not in the world only for itself. We are also here for the sake of the lost. The church is meant to be engaged with the world, not huddled in isolation. The quality of our relationships is a primary way that God reveals himself to the lost world.

Study 29: Our Call to Engage the World

JOHN 17:20-26

As you sent me into the world, I have sent them into the world. For them I sanctify myself, that they too may be truly sanctified. My prayer is not for them alone. I pray also for those who will believe in me through their message, that all of them may be one, Father, just as you are in me and I am in you. May they also be in us so that the world may believe that you have sent me. I have given them the glory that you gave me, that they may be one as we are one—I in them and you in me—so that they may be brought to complete unity. Then the world will know that you sent me and have loved them even as you have loved me. Father, I want those you have given me to be with me where I am, and to see my glory, the glory you have given me because you loved me before the creation of the world. Righteous Father, though the world does not know you, I know you, and they know that you have sent me. I have made you known to them, and will continue to make you known in order that the love you have for me may be in them and that I myself may be in them.

1 PETER 2:9-12

But you are a chosen people, a royal priesthood, a holy nation, God's special possession, that you may declare the praises of him who called you out of darkness into his wonderful light. Once you were not a people, but now you are the people of God; once you had not received mercy, but now you have received mercy. Dear friends, I urge you, as foreigners and exiles, to abstain from sinful desires, which wage war against your soul. Live such good lives among the pagans that, though they accuse you of doing wrong, they may see your good deeds and glorify God on the day he visits us.

Think Deeper

29.1 How can the people of God relate well with each other while also being engaged relationally with the lost?

Ekklesia: Diverse Forms and Actions

Throughout the New Testament, we see communities of believers actively serving one another and spreading the Gospel across cultures and generations. In the New Testament, the word *ekklesia* is used in a variety of ways. For example, in Romans 16, Paul uses the word to refer to a city-wide church, a household church, and a regional church. In all of these cases, the church is people, not the meeting location. In Section 2, we saw that the Gospel advanced through families, the household, or *oikos*. One expression of *ekklesia* commonly seen around the world today includes formal and traditional elements such as special buildings, liturgy, choirs, and pastors or priests. In other places, *ekklesia* is commonly expressed as families and networks of friends coming together in homes and sharing life together.

Study 30: New Testament Expressions of Church

Acts 13:1-5

Now in the church at Antioch there were prophets and teachers: Barnabas, Simeon called Niger, Lucius of Cyrene, Manaen (who had been brought up with Herod the tetrarch) and Saul. While they were worshiping the Lord and fasting, the Holy Spirit said, "Set apart for me Barnabas and Saul for the work to which I have called them." So after they had fasted and prayed, they placed their hands on them and sent them off. The two of them, sent on their way by the Holy Spirit, went down to Seleucia and sailed from there to Cyprus. When they arrived at Salamis, they proclaimed the word of God in the Jewish synagogues. John was with them as their helper.

Acts 4:31-35

After they prayed, the place where they were meeting was shaken. And they were all filled with the Holy Spirit and spoke the word of God boldly. All the believers were one in heart and mind. No one claimed that any of their possessions was their own, but they shared everything they had. With great power the apostles continued to testify to the resurrection of the Lord Jesus. And God's grace was so powerfully at work in them all that there were no needy persons among them. For from time to time those who owned land or houses sold them, brought the money from the sales and put it at the apostles' feet, and it was distributed to anyone who had need.

GALATIANS 2:9

James, Cephas and John, those esteemed as pillars, gave me and Barnabas the right hand of fellowship when they recognized the grace given to me.

PHILIPPIANS 1:5

. . . because of your partnership in the gospel from the first day until now . . .

1 THESSALONIANS 1:2-3

We always thank God for all of you and continually mention you in our prayers. We remember before our God and Father your work produced by faith, your labor prompted by love, and your endurance inspired by hope in our Lord Jesus Christ.

2 THESSALONIANS 4:9-12

Now about your love for one another we do not need to write to you, for you yourselves have been taught by God to love each other. And in fact, you do love all of God's family throughout Macedonia. Yet we urge you . . . to do so more and more, and to make it your ambition to lead a quiet life: You should mind your own business and work with your hands, just as we told you, so that your daily life may win the respect of outsiders and so that you will not be dependent on anybody.

Think Deeper

30.1 What does serving together do for the ability of an *ekklesia* to thrive internally and impact the world?

30.2 What could *ekklesia* look like in the culture to which you are going? What forms might work best for discipleship and outreach among the lost?

A Case Study

Over a few years in "Metropolis," a number of young people from a Buddhist background in their 20s and 30s came to Christ. Many of them are friends or related as family. They get together regularly to study the Bible and seek counsel from one another.

They are told by other Christian friends that they ought to go to a nearby church. They don't mind going on Sundays, but they ask why they need to go to church when they are growing in Christ together and relating to unreached family members and friends who do not want to go to church.

These young believers are not sure what to do. Is the group a valid church? Do they need to do anything more in order to be "church"? If so, what? How would you advise them to relate with the people who invited them to church?

A Case Study

Raja (not his real name), who is from a devout family of a major non-Christian religion, came to Christ after a few years reading the Scriptures with Christian friends. When he made known his faith, he was heavily persecuted.

Sometime later, his younger brother also came to faith. They agreed that the younger brother would keep his decision to follow Christ private for a time. The two of them, together with the person who loved them into the kingdom, got together weekly to study the Scriptures, to pray, and to encourage one another.

Raja and his brother are praying for the rest of their family to come to Christ. They are also praying for people in their ethnic relational network to know Jesus. How would you advise Raja and his brother about what church should look like for them? What are your reasons?

DISCIPLESHIP IN COMMUNITY

We turn now to the importance of community as this pertains to the spiritual development of men and women. Transformed lives are the basis for healthy communities and communities are essential for the effective transformation of people. They are interdependent.

Bartimaeus, the blind man who encountered the Lord barely a week before he died on the cross, was considered a "disciple." Paul was also a disciple. And so were Lydia of Philippi and the Samaritan lady of John 4. Some were Jews, others were Samaritans, Cretans, or Greeks. Some were young in their faith and others had walked with Jesus for much longer. Some were apostles, evangelists, or teachers. Some functioned as elders or deacons; others were ordinary saints in Christ who had a quiet but powerful impact. However, there are some essential qualities of a disciple.

Study 31: What Is a Disciple?

LUKE 9:23

Then he said to them all: "Whoever wants to be my disciple must deny themselves and take up their cross daily and follow me."

JOHN 8:31-32

To the Jews who had believed him, Jesus said, "If you hold to my teaching, you are really my disciples. Then you will know the truth, and the truth will set you free."

JOHN 13:34-35

A new command I give you: Love one another. As I have loved you, so you must love one another. By this everyone will know that you are my disciples, if you love one another.

JOHN 15:7-8

If you remain in me and my words remain in you, ask whatever you wish, and it will be done for you. This is to my Father's glory, that you bear much fruit, showing yourselves to be my disciples.

Think Deeper

31.1 Based on the scriptures above, what word for "disciple" would work well among the lost in your culture?

SPIRITUAL TRANSFORMATION AND COMMUNITY

True transformation happens when God inhabits the natural self. Spiritual transformation takes place best in the context of deep relationships. Navigators call this "life-on-life discipleship." This can take place as community is expressed in the course of daily work, family, raising children, and marriage.

People need to belong to a network of relationships who are committed to one another, to God, and to his purposes. We can't grow in Christ in isolation. We need the benefits of the entire body to grow fully, and the body needs us.

Dietrich Bonhoeffer, in his book *Life Together,* said, "He who is alone with his sin is utterly alone. . . . The pious fellowship permits no one to be a sinner. In confession, the breakthrough to community takes place. Sin demands to have a man by himself, it withdraws him from community. The more isolated a person is, the more destructive will be the power of sin over him."

Study 32: Examples of Life-on-Life Discipleship

MARK 1:29-39

As soon as they left the synagogue, they went with James and John to the home of Simon and Andrew. Simon's mother-in-law was in bed with a fever, and they immediately told Jesus about her. So he went to her, took her hand and helped her up. The fever left her and she began to wait on them. That evening after sunset the people brought to Jesus all the sick and demon-possessed. The whole town gathered at the door, and Jesus healed many who had various diseases. He also drove out many demons, but he would not let the demons speak because they knew who he was. Very early in the morning, while it was still dark, Jesus got up, left the house and went off to a solitary place, where he prayed. Simon and his companions went to look for him, and when they found him, they exclaimed: "Everyone is looking for you!" Jesus replied, "Let us go somewhere else—to the nearby villages—so I can preach there also. That is why I have come." So he traveled throughout Galilee, preaching in their synagogues and driving out demons.

JOHN 11:5-6, 33-36 (DEATH OF LAZARUS)

Jesus loved Martha and her sister and Lazarus. Yet when he heard Lazarus was sick, he stayed where he was two more days. . . . When Jesus saw her (Mary) weeping, and the Jews who had come along with her also weeping, he was deeply moved in spirit and troubled. "Where have you laid him?" he asked. "Come and see, Lord," they replied. Jesus wept. Then the Jews said, "See how he loved him!"

COLOSSIANS 3:12-21

Therefore, as God's chosen people, holy and dearly loved, clothe yourselves with compassion, kindness, humility, gentleness and patience. Bear with each other and forgive one another if any of you has a grievance against someone. Forgive as the Lord forgave you. And over all these virtues put on love, which binds them all together in perfect unity. Let the peace of Christ rule in your hearts, since as members of one body you were called to peace. And be thankful. Let the message of Christ dwell among you richly as you teach and admonish one another with all wisdom through psalms, hymns, and songs from the Spirit, singing to God with gratitude in your hearts. And whatever you do, whether in word or deed, do it all in the name of the Lord Jesus, giving thanks to God the Father through him. Wives, submit yourselves to your husbands, as is fitting in the Lord. Husbands, love your wives and do not be harsh with them. Children, obey your parents in everything, for this pleases the Lord. Fathers, do not embitter your children, or they will become discouraged.

Think Deeper

32.1 Notice how first-century believers saw all of life as church. What dynamics of normal life in *ekklesia* can aid life-on-life discipling?

ℭℛ

Study 33: Spiritual Transformation and Walking in the Light

JOHN 3:19-21

This is the verdict: Light has come into the world, but people loved darkness instead of light because their deeds were evil. Everyone who does evil hates the light, and will not come into the light for fear that their deeds will be exposed. But whoever lives by the truth comes into the light, so that it may be seen plainly that what they have done has been done in the sight of God.

JAMES 5:16

Therefore, confess your sins to each other and pray for each other so that you may be healed.

1 JOHN 1:5-9

This is the message we have heard from him and declare to you: God is light; in him there is no darkness at all. If we claim to have fellowship with him and yet walk in the darkness, we lie and do not live out the truth. But if we walk in the light, as he is in the light, we have fellowship with one another, and the blood of Jesus, his Son, purifies us from all sin. If we claim to be without sin, we deceive ourselves and the truth is not in us. If we confess our sins, he is faithful and just and will forgive us our sins and purify us from all unrighteousness.

Discover More

Believers can experience God's involvement in times of need, pain, and struggle with sin. Explore the following scriptures: Genesis 16; Hebrews 11:24-27; Isaiah 6:2-8; Philippians 3:8-11.

Think Deeper

33.1 What is the relationship between a safe community and spiritual transformation? How can a safe community serve non-believing friends?

A Case Study

Imagine you are a cross-cultural missionary called to pioneer a campus ministry in country that has a long Navigator history. The city where you are starting to reach students has a group of Navigator believers. You are close to them and they are supporting your efforts. As new students come to Christ, they are hesitant to engage with the existing local group because the relationships are not natural. On the one hand, the students would benefit from the maturity of the larger group. On the other hand, the students have their own friends, many of whom are not believers. What would you do and why?

SPIRITUAL TRANSFORMATION AND THE CROSS

Surrender, humility, and obedience undergird the disciplines of spiritual transformation. The Holy Spirit, prayer, the Word, and relationships are powerful tools for spiritual transformation. Because of the cross of Jesus, our progress is shaped by each person's humility before Jesus and trust in him.

Study 34: Living a New Life

ROMANS 6:1-11

What shall we say, then? Shall we go on sinning so that grace may increase? By no means! We are those who have died to sin; how can we live in it any longer? Or don't you know that all of us who were baptized into Christ Jesus were baptized into his death? We were therefore buried with him through baptism into death in order that, just as Christ was raised from the dead through the glory of the Father, we too may live a new life. For if we have been united with him in a death like his, we will certainly also be united with him in a resurrection like his. For we know that our old self was crucified with him so that the body ruled by sin might be done away with, that we should no longer be slaves to sin, because anyone who has died has been set free from sin. Now if we died with Christ, we believe that we will also live with him. For we know that since Christ was raised from the dead, he cannot die again; death no longer has mastery over him. The death he died, he died to sin once for all; but the life he lives, he lives to God. In the same way, count yourselves dead to sin but alive to God in Christ Jesus.

1 PETER 2:24-25

He himself bore our sins" in his body on the cross, so that we might die to sins and live for righteousness; "by his wounds you have been healed." For "you were like sheep going astray," but now you have returned to the Shepherd and Overseer of your souls.

Think Deeper

34.1 How does the cross restore broken people and relationships?

WORKING WITH BROKEN PEOPLE

Study 35: The Power of the Gospel to Heal Troubled Souls

MARK 7:20-23

What comes out of a person is what defiles them. For it is from within, out of a person's heart, that evil thoughts come—sexual immorality, theft, murder, adultery, greed, malice, deceit, lewdness, envy, slander, arrogance and folly. All these evils come from inside and defile a person.

1 CORINTHIANS 6:9-11

Or do you not know that wrongdoers will not inherit the kingdom of God? Do not be deceived: Neither the sexually immoral nor idolaters nor adulterers nor men who have sex with men nor thieves nor the greedy nor drunkards nor slanderers nor swindlers will inherit the kingdom of God. And that is what some of you were. But you were washed, you were sanctified, you were justified in the name of the Lord Jesus Christ and by the Spirit of our God.

GALATIANS 5:16-25

So I say, walk by the Spirit, and you will not gratify the desires of the flesh. For the flesh desires what is contrary to the Spirit, and the Spirit what is contrary to the flesh. They are in conflict with each other, so that you are not to do whatever you want. But if you are led by the Spirit, you are not under the law. The acts of the flesh are obvious: sexual immorality, impurity and debauchery; idolatry and witchcraft; hatred, discord, jealousy, fits of rage, selfish ambition, dissensions, factions and envy; drunkenness, orgies, and the like. . . . But the fruit of the Spirit is love, joy, peace, forbearance, kindness, goodness, faithfulness, gentleness and self-control. . . . Those who belong to Christ Jesus have crucified the flesh with its passions and desires. Since we live by the Spirit, let us keep in step with the Spirit.

ROMANS 8:1-5

Therefore, there is now no condemnation for those who are in Christ Jesus, because through Christ Jesus the law of the Spirit who gives life has set you free from the law of sin and death. For what the law was powerless to do because it was weakened by the flesh, God did by sending his own Son in the likeness of sinful flesh to be a sin offering. And so he condemned sin in the flesh, in order that the righteous requirement of the law might be fully met in us, who do not live according to the flesh but according to the Spirit. Those who live according to the flesh have their minds set on what the flesh desires; but those who live in accordance with the Spirit have their minds set on what the Spirit desires.

Think Deeper

35.1 Why is the Gospel so powerful for transforming lives? What is each person's responsibility in the process of transformation?

A Case Study

In Southeast Asia, a woman possessed by demons was cast out of a village after she killed one of her children by burying the child alive. The woman lived in a nearby forest, alone and deranged. Then she returned and did the same thing to one of her other children. She had extraordinary physical strength for a woman her size and age, and was seen breaking large limbs off trees with one arm. The people in the town were terrified of her.

A local man who had been discipled by Navigators decided to help the woman and the people in his village. He wanted to get his guidance from the Scriptures. So he carefully studied how Jesus handled demons in Mark 5:1-20. Basing his actions on Jesus's model, he confronted the possessed woman and healed her. The people in the town moved closer to Christ as a result. Read Mark 5:1-20 and determine what you would do if you were in the Asian man's shoes. (Refer also to the section about spiritual warfare on page 46-50.)

TRANSFORMED BY GOD'S WORD AND SPIRIT

Discipleship also requires involvement with the Word and with the Holy Spirit. Unfortunately, in our busy and distracted times, people are spending less time in God's Word and in prayer. This tendency can lead people to grow old but not up. We need God's Word and Spirit to speak into our lives. Without them we can mix the Gospel with the surrounding culture and remain blind to our own sin.

Study 36: How God's Word and Spirit Work Together

PSALM 119:105
Your word is a lamp for my feet, a light on my path.

2 TIMOTHY 3:16-17
All scripture is God-breathed and is useful for teaching, rebuking, correcting

and training in righteousness, so that the servant of God may be thoroughly equipped for every good work.

Hebrews 4:12

For the word of God is alive and active. Sharper than any double-edged sword, it penetrates even to dividing soul and spirit, joints and marrow; it judges the thoughts and attitudes of the heart.

John 16:13

But when he, the Spirit of truth, comes, he will guide you into all the truth. He will not speak on his own; he will speak only what he hears, and he will tell you what is yet to come.

1 Corinthians 2:12-14

What we have received is not the spirit of the world, but the Spirit who is from God, so that we may understand what God has freely given us. This is what we speak, not in words taught us by human wisdom but in words taught by the Spirit, explaining spiritual realities with Spirit-taught words. The person without the Spirit does not accept the things that come from the Spirit of God but considers them foolishness, and cannot understand them because they are discerned only through the Spirit.

Galatians 5:16-18, 25

So I say, live by the Spirit, and you will not gratify the desires of the sinful nature. For the sinful nature desires what is contrary to the Spirit, and the Spirit what is contrary to the sinful nature. They are in conflict with each other, so that you do not do what you want. But if you are led by the Spirit, you are not under law. . . . Since we live by the Spirit, let us keep in step with the Spirit.

Discover More

To understand more about the role of the Holy Spirit, please read Luke 11:13; 1 Corinthians 12:7-11.

Think Deeper

36.1 What are some barriers today that prevent people from engaging with the Bible? How can we help them overcome these barriers?

36.2 How should the Holy Spirit's work in people affect the way we think about our involvement with them?

A Case Study

Bala met Christ and The Navigators as a first-year university student. He joined a small-group Bible study and started spending time with the leader. Through these initiatives, Bala learned to have a quiet time, to study the Bible, and to share his faith. He began to clean up some negative behaviors such as language, womanizing, and hanging out with bad company. By the time he graduated, Bala had embraced the Navigator vision of discipleship and spiritual multiplication, but he also lost contact with his non-Christian friends.

As a young professional, Bala stayed connected to Navigators and got married to Alice. They became busy at work, with Navigator ministry, and at church. But at work, Bala had a bad reputation. People experienced him as snobbish and judgmental. Very few people wanted to be close to him. He was living beyond his means at the expense of other people. Memorization, Navigator meetings, and other practices began to feel legalistic. What do you observe to be the gaps in Bala's spiritual development? How would you disciple Bala differently?

THE SOVEREIGNTY OF GOD

At the beginning of the this study, we focused on the key promises that God has given to Navigators over the course of our history. Indeed, God has done more than we could ask or imagine, and we fully expect that he will continue to work powerfully to expand his kingdom through the generations.

The apostle John, in Revelation 7:9, gives us a glimpse of what God's sovereign plan will look like, ultimately, in eternity. "After this I looked and there before me was a great multitude that no one could count, from every nation, tribe, people and language, standing before the throne and in front of the Lamb."

By faith we work toward this vision. But the outcomes of our efforts to reach the nations are not always immediately visible. We have an important influence, but we are not in control of the results. Sometimes the ultimate results of investing in people show up much later. Therefore, we need to trust God's sovereignty, knowing that our "work in the Lord will not be in vain" (1 Corinthians 15:58). We live by faith, believing in God and his promises.

Study 37: Understanding God's Role and Our Role

ISAIAH 64:8

Yet you, Lord, are our Father. We are the clay, you are the potter; we are all the work of your hand.

MATTHEW 13

Listen then to what the parable of the sower means: When anyone hears the message about the kingdom and does not understand it, the evil one comes and snatches away what was sown in their heart. This is the seed sown along the path. The seed falling on rocky ground refers to someone who hears the word and at once receives it with joy. But since they have no root, they last only a short time. When trouble or persecution comes because of the word, they quickly fall away. The seed falling among the thorns refers to someone who hears the word, but the worries of this life and the deceitfulness of wealth choke the word, making it unfruitful. But the seed falling on good soil refers to someone who hears the word and understands it. This is the one who produces a crop, yielding a hundred, sixty or thirty times what was sown.

LUKE 10:2

He told them, "The harvest is plentiful, but the workers are few. Ask the Lord of the harvest, therefore, to send out workers into his harvest field."

JOHN 4:38

I sent you to reap what you have not worked for. Others have done the hard work, and you have reaped the benefits of their labor.

1 CORINTHIANS 3:5-15

What, after all, is Apollos? And what is Paul? Only servants, through whom you came to believe—as the Lord has assigned to each his task. I planted the seed, Apollos watered it, but God has been making it grow. So neither the one who plants nor the one who waters is anything, but only God, who makes things grow. The one who plants and the one who waters have one purpose, and they will each be rewarded according to their own labor. For we are co-workers in God's service; you are God's field, God's building.

By the grace God has given me, I laid a foundation as a wise builder, and someone else is building on it. But each one should build with care. For no one can lay any foundation other than the one already laid, which is Jesus Christ. If anyone builds on this foundation using gold, silver, costly stones, wood, hay or straw, their work will be shown for what it is, because the Day will bring it to light. It will be revealed with fire, and the fire will test the quality of each person's work. If what has been built survives, the builder will receive a reward. If it is burned up, the builder will suffer loss but yet will be saved—even though only as one escaping through the flames.

HEBREWS 11:1-2

Now faith is confidence in what we hope for and assurance about what we do not see. This is what the ancients were commended for. . . .

Thinking Deeper

37.1 Based on the Scriptures above, how would you summarize our responsibility as cross-cultural servants of the Gospel? What is God's role as the "Lord of the harvest"?

37.2 As a cross-cultural laborer, how would you know that the work the Lord has assigned you has been fulfilled?

A Case Study

After many years of faithful service among lost people in a major religion, a Navigator couple had formed strong friendships and had faithfully shared their faith in both life and word. However, they did not see any evidence that their ministry was bearing fruit. No one had accepted their invitations to read the Scriptures, and no one seemed to be moving toward a relationship with Jesus. This cross-cultural couple began to wonder if they should change their approach to ministry. Deep in their hearts, they also wondered if they should end their work in that region. This thought, however, conflicted with their love for the people and their hope in God's power. How would you counsel them in these decisions? How would you encourage them?

LIVING BY FAITH

By Mutua Mahiaini

As cross-cultural missionaries serving around the world, some will work among the poor and oppressed in urban and rural areas. Others will reach out to young men and women on college campuses. Still others will carry the Gospel into the business world. In all these endeavors, we need to keep our eyes focused on our overarching calling and purpose. We are, above all, servants of the Gospel of Jesus and his kingdom.

Paul, writing in Ephesians 3:7-9, says: "I became a servant of this gospel by the gift of God's grace given me through the working of his power. Although I am less than the least of all the Lord's people, this grace was given me: to preach to the Gentiles the boundless riches of Christ, and to make plain to everyone the administration of this mystery, which for ages past was kept hidden in God, who created all things."

Paul was convinced of the Gospel's power. He knew that it was the most important message in history. He knew that its source, Jesus, was Lord of all, king of kings. Thus, the Gospel had authority over Paul's life. His own life and well-being was subservient to the eternal purpose of God and his love for people as expressed in the Gospel message.

Paul was not a grumbling servant; rather, he was joyful. For him, to be a servant of the Gospel was a "gift of God's grace." He acknowledged that he had done nothing to earn this gift when he says, "I am less than the least of all the Lord's people." To give his life in service to the Gospel was a privilege.

We also learn from Paul that serving as cross-cultural servants of the Gospel is not ultimately about how educated we are, or how creative our ministry methods might be, or how gifted we are at speaking. Paul says, "For I resolved to know nothing while I was with you except Jesus Christ and him crucified. I came to you in weakness and fear, and with much trembling. My message and my preaching were not with wise and persuasive words, but with a demonstration of the Spirit's power, so that your faith might not rest on men's wisdom, but on God's power" (1 Corinthians 2:2-5).

Convinced of God's sovereignty, filled with a godly passion for the Gospel and a sincere love for people, Paul was willing to go through prison, hunger, shipwrecks, and death threats without giving up. "To live is Christ and to die is gain," he said. The Gospel calls us to persevere because we know it will not fail. As Isaiah 55:10-11 says, "As the rain and the snow come down from heaven, and do not return to it without watering the earth and making it bud and flourish . . . so is my word that goes out from my mouth; It will not return to me empty, but will accomplish what I desire and achieve the purspose for which I sent it."

Paul also shows us that God's work to advance the Gospel into the nations is far greater than The Navigators. We are humble partners in a grand orchestra conducted by God. Paul stated this clearly, using agricultural terms, in 1 Corinthians 3:6, which says: "I planted the seed, Apollos watered it, but God made it grow."

All this requires faith! As we follow Christ into cross-cultural missions, it is crucial for us to foster a culture of faith in our personal lives, in our ministries, and in our teams. Faith is what God wants from us! Hebrews 11:6 says, "without faith it is impossible to please God." And in Luke 18, Jesus asked: "When the Son of Man comes, will he find faith on the earth?"

Faith helps us thrive in three ways. First, the world is changing; because each generation presents new challenges, faith spurs us to serve people in ways that might be quite different than what has been done in the past. Faith challenges us to be innovative, to take risks, to try new things. We, as Navigators, should look to God's leading, not just maintain traditions.

Second, when God's people live by faith, we become people of hope! Hope is something that other people can see and experience. Peter wrote, "But in your hearts revere Christ as Lord. Always be prepared to give an answer to everyone who asks you to give the reason for the hope that you have." Hope, Paul says, should be so visible in our lives that people will come and ask us why we are so hopeful!

Third, faith produces unity. In faith, we are all worshiping and submitting our lives to Jesus. Our humility before God reduces prideful tendencies that lead to conflict and division. The Worldwide Partnership of The Navigators is incredibly diverse, but as we worship together in faith we experience increasing unity—even across cultures and languages.

How do we sustain and expand a culture of faith in our lives and work?

A culture of faith grows from one source: Jesus. It emerges and is sustained as people focus on him, looking to his glory, trusting him in all circumstances. As we give our lives to cross-cultural service of the Gospel, Psalm 34:1-3 reminds us that our work is about God, not us. "I will extol the Lord at all times; his praise will always be on my lips. I will glory in the Lord; let the afflicted hear and rejoice. Glorify the Lord with me; let us exalt his name together."

Serving with you,
Mutua Mahiaini
International President

Made in the USA
Charleston, SC
23 October 2016